the anxiety diaries

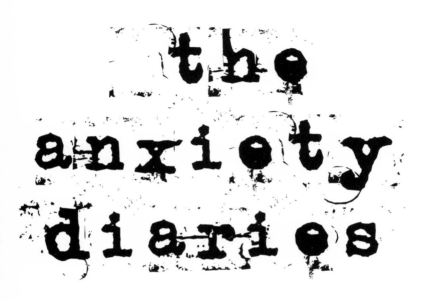

the anxiety diaries

VOLUME ONE

DANA MUWWAKKIL

THE ANXIETY DIARIES: VOLUME 1

This book is a work of non-fiction, based on true
events as recorded in the author's personal diary. Any
similarities to other works are coincidental.

THE ANXIETY DIARIES: VOLUME 1 © 2020 Dana Muwwakkil

ISBN-13: 978-0-578-72932-9

Published by Dana Muwwakkil
Marlboro, NY

Printed in the United States of America
First Edition September 2020

Cover Design by Komal Chandwani, Mindscape Designs
Interior Layout by Make Your Mark Publishing Solutions
Editing by Make Your Mark Publishing Solutions

For Irshaad

CONTENTS

ACKNOWLEDGEMENTS

First and foremost, I would like to thank my husband, Irshaad, for his support and believing in this book and believing in me. I want to thank Monique and Make Your Mark Publishing Solutions for helping me bring this diary to life. To Komal at Mindscape Designs, thank you for your patience and creativity and for designing such a dope cover for me.

To Bethanni, thank you for being my best friend and support system. Mom, thank you for helping me stay sane and being there when I needed it. Dad, thank you for understanding and for your support; it means so much to me. To Andrea, thanks for making me laugh when I felt like crying and for understanding. To Ricky, thank you for being my big brother and for listening. To Amanda, thank you for all your advice, your input, and help. I want to thank Shea, Krystal, Idris, and Marquis from "The Inkwell" for being the first people to read *The Anxiety Diaries* and for their encouragement to keep writing it. To Ms. Felicia, thank you for giving me my first real writing gig and believing in me. To Samantha, Jane, and Lisa, thank you for being supportive, and to my mental health providers, thank you for your patience and kindness. To all my online friends whom I have connected with during this journey, thank you for listening to my story and for rooting for me.

Lastly, I would like to thank the reader. Thank you for picking up this book and helping my dreams of becoming an author turn into reality.

Peace and Love,
Dana

"I'll tell you what Freedom is to me. No fear."
-Nina Simone

january

2019

Currently

MAKING my new planner

LOVING a fresh start

WATCHING my baby grow up fast

READING my own works

LISTENING to the baby snore

EATING tacos

DRINKING water and coffee

HATING my anxiety

WANTING peace

THINKING about my future

PLANNING to be a better me

WISHING for strength

1.1.2019

Good morning, world! I am working on my new planner, which I am DIYing (hopefully, I can stick with it this year). I'm so excited for 2019 and all it may bring.

1.2.2019

My planner is in full effect! Today is chaotic, getting used to the school and workweek again. Home with the two youngest. I worked out, and I feel good. Finally attempted to make an appointment to see my psychiatrist. Gotta start the process all over again and see the therapist first. I think it's bullshit, but I didn't fight it. I have never been a rule breaker. Sometimes I wish I was.

1.3.2019

Productive day, although I was so tired. It's only the third day of the year, but I'm feeling good so far. Baby sis called me crying today because she was confronted with more evidence that the "man" she loves ain't shit. It was brutal, but I hope she finally walks away. Stay tuned.

1.4.2019

I have so many things I wish to achieve this year.

- Being featured in a specific publication with other talented black writers

- Getting family portraits done
- Finally going on a vacation
- Getting more in tune with yoga and meditation
- Self-publishing something this year
- Staying in my truth
- Getting *fit*, not losing weight

This is the year of yes—or no if it has to be.

1.5.2019

Nice day. We went out as a family, which is rare. Did some shopping, had yummy food, and my anxiety didn't fuck with me. Going to be busy tomorrow, but that's OK. My incision is hurting. My *last* C-section really fucked me up. Emphasis on "last!"

1.6.2019

Stressful, long, sad day. I feel powerless, full of so many words that want to come out but won't. I feel like I will never live up to my potential. Baby is four months old today. Tomorrow, mom is four months sober. I have a busy and definitely stressful week ahead. I'm going to keep it moving, though.

1.7.2019

Pushing myself out of my comfort zone means being confrontational, even when I don't want to be. I'm twenty-eight and want to be liked so badly; it's utterly pathetic. I've been a people pleaser all my life. That has got to change.

1.8.2019

I don't know what to write. I meditated this morning. Don't know when I will be able to again because getting alone time in this house is *hard*. Anyway, my mantra is to be positive today. I did have a good day. I'm just so damn tired. Goodnight.

1.9.2019

I found the time to meditate this morning and do some quick yoga. I feel good. I need to write, but my soul still feels stifled, like the words can't come out. I read someone's story in my writer's group, and it was so well written. I really need to step my game up. I can tell it came from, not just pure talent, but hard work and discipline.

1.10.2019

Speaking up for myself is probably one of the hardest challenges I face. My oldest is a lot like me, passive. That's why I'm already pushing her out of her comfort zone and forcing her to speak up for herself. I don't want her to be like me.

1.11.2019

Feeling low today, like my energy and optimism for the new year has already dissipated. I want a real break, but I know I shouldn't complain. I'm blessed. I need to start a gratitude thread.

1.12.2019

I want to be great so, so badly. I want to feel good about myself. I want to be energized, happy, and passionate. I want to be better so badly, it brings tears to my eyes.

1.13.2019

Sunday. Getting ready for another week. Feeling positive. I had a break and did some self-care last night. It's paying off today. Ready for the cycle of alarm clocks, backpacks, and having my baby constantly on my boob to continue once again. I'm going to try meditation and yoga early in the morning. It's my only option if I want to do it alone.

1.14.2019

Today, I chose meditation and yoga over an extra hour of sleep. I must be crazy. Somehow, I was able to get housework done, and I finally have a few moments to myself. I had my writer's meeting last night, and I really need to get my ass in gear. I have been writing but nothing structured, just ramblings, incoherent thoughts, and unfinished poems. Better get on it.

1.15.2019

I feel *fucking great*!

1.16.2019

My writer's group is putting together an anthology, and although I've been MIA for a long time, they are allowing me to contribute. I'm working on the foreword right now, and I'm already excited. I just don't know why it's so hard for me to have the same enthusiasm for my own projects. I have to keep challenging myself. I guess it's just hard when I'm the only one holding myself accountable. I also had a chance to do yoga or sleep again today. I chose to sleep this time, and I'm glad I did.

1.17.2019

I was having some scary thoughts today, but I chose to block them and focus on Miyah's birthday. I have some rather ambitious plans for Miyah's sixth birthday on Tuesday and her party the following Saturday. Rainbow cake from scratch and rainbow cupcakes for school, homemade rainbow tutus for her and her sisters, and a birthday cake headband that may be a fail. I can't wait to see her face on her day. I love being a mommy, and I love making my children feel special and beautiful.

1.18.2019

I don't know why, but I'm still surprised when my husband comes home from work early sometimes or has an unusual day off and I don't get the "break" from my kids I was expecting. And I must be fair, he is out of the house a lot—right now about fifty-five hours a week—and he has errands to run and stuff he wants to do, too. I understand it. To give myself a little break, I decided to lay here while the baby is sleeping instead of doing any house chores or anything on my to-do list. I might pay for it later, but I think this hour of peace will be worth it.

1.19.2019

Hubby is home today. I really did have a good day with my husband and girls. I've been missing Irshaad so much. It's nice to just be around each other.

1.20.2019

Another week has gone by, and this one was a really great week. I stuck to my goals, I ate right (even in the face of temptation that is my husband's pies and cakes), I got in a couple of light workouts, and most of all, I kept a pretty positive attitude. I had a great day, but it was really long, and I was involved with doing Miyah's hair for her birthday. I really want her day to be wonderful. My baby deserves to feel special and awesome. I am nervous about the cake, though.

1.21.2019

There are never enough minutes in the day. I've been prepping for Miyah's birthday tomorrow all weekend, washing, blow-drying, and flat-ironing hair, baking, and getting balloons and decor. I still have to wrap presents and blow up balloons. I was completely stressed out and bitchy today. I'm going to be just as stressed tomorrow because of the damn cake from scratch I wanted to make. Fingers crossed it tastes good and is aesthetically pleasing. I can't wait to see Miyah's smiling face tomorrow.

1.22.2019

What an incredible and incredibly long day! Miyah had a great day, and I cannot believe my first daughter is six freaking years old! I did my best to make sure she felt loved and awesome from the moment she woke up in a bedroom full of balloons. She looked so darling in her dress, which eventually became covered (and probably ruined) in spaghetti sauce and other foods, and that is absolutely OK.

The rainbow cake, my very first cake from scratch, looked awesome and was a hit—well, almost. I'm a little disappointed after all the effort that went into making Miyah's cake that she wasn't a fan of the frosting, saying, "Mommy, it's yucky." Not sure why I decided to do a cream cheese one and not just keep it all vanilla. I was kind of upset about it until Bethanni made me feel better, reminding me that I worked my ass off and should be proud. At least now I have a go-to vanilla cake. Now, I just need a chocolate one.

1.23.2019

I had a rare window of time when both Aaliyah and Angel were napping, and I decided to take full advantage by doing a very intense core yoga workout. It was awesome. Although I've dropped back to my pre-baby weight, I cannot get into any of my jeans comfortably, partly because my C-section area is still very tender. I'm very pleased because I've been losing about a pound a week, and I'm pretty happy with how I have been disciplining myself by eating clean and doing light workouts when I can. I really believe it's helping my mood and even my anxiety.

1.24.2019

I really don't feel like writing anything today, like, I am really pushing myself to write just this. Let's see, I took Miyah to the doctor today. Her stomach had been hurting her a lot. I have to get an ultrasound done for her, which is kind of frightening but just a formality, I suppose. I think it might be a dairy intolerance. We shall see. Today went by quickly. I was busy and didn't make time to work out. I will try and get in another workout tomorrow.

1.25.2019

The month is coming to a close. I am proud that I have been able to *be consistent* with eating clean. I think I have finally mentally come to a place where I am ready to feel better and, let's be honest, *look* better. I still can't get into any of my jeans as of right now, and that's OK. My scar is still tender as hell, and my stomach has an extra flap of skin hanging over it. I am only twenty-eight! I am in the prime of my life. I want to look like it. And so, it shall be done.

1.26.2019

Birthday party for my Miyah today, and she is having her very first sleepover at home. Then, all the birthday madness will be behind us, although Valentine's Day is right around the corner. I want to get Irshaad something he will really like. My gifts, although always thoughtful, can be hit or miss. I already ordered him some earrings I know he will like, but it's not enough. I wish I could spoil the shit out of that man. He deserves it. Maybe one day, we won't be poor anymore, living paycheck to paycheck while trying desperately to save but at the same time wanting to have fun and eat good and do things. No matter how much money he makes, it's never enough. Never.

1.27.2019

Writer's meeting went well. Feedback for the foreword I wrote ranged from "I loved it!" to "It was good" to "I didn't really get a chance to read the whole thing." I'm pleased it was well received by my peers because all the writers in my group (there are five of us, all black) are so effing talented. I'm in such good company, and I still have much to learn about my craft.

It's Sunday, and I was busy all day. Irshaad and I got into a heated argument over a TV show, and I got so insanely mad. I don't know why. I see my therapist again next week.

1.28.2019

Every day is different, yet every day is more or less the same. Sometimes I feel so trapped in this cycle of monotony. Not much changes for me on my end, especially during the weekdays. But then, it's like that for a lot of people, most probably. With school and work, isn't it all different yet the same? I see my peers on social media. I see them jetting off to foreign places, having fun and being young. Sometimes I have to remind myself that I am still a young person. I love my life. I love my children. I love my husband. They are my world. Sometimes I get lonely, and sometimes I want to put myself first. Once in a while, I get the opportunity to do so. To be honest, I feel guilty even wanting a social life. My husband barely has one, too. That's just the way it goes.

1.29.2019

My mood is complete shit today. The kids are home from school for a snow day, and I'm irritated by their presence. Moms aren't supposed to say these things. Yes, I signed up for this. I know that. I'm still a human. I'm also a little aggravated for other reasons.

- I made myself a really disgusting salad for lunch and followed it with chocolate and a bagel, which made me feel like I ruined my caloric intake for the day.
- I'm stressing over my foreword, which I have edited to include things about the anthology, and it doesn't feel like the beautiful love letter I first wrote for my

Dana Muwwakkil

daughters. I haven't found the sweet spot yet to make it feel right.
- I have appointments looming next week and no car to get to them. Irshaad has been using my car since something is *always* wrong with his.

I think I'm going to get out alone this weekend, maybe on Friday evening. I hate feeling overwhelmed this way. It makes me a mean wife and a mean mom.

1.30.2019

I got to work out and do yoga today, and I was still in a shitty mood most of the day. I fixed my foreword, and I love it again. I was disciplined AF, doing the things that are supposed to help me feel good, and I was *still* in a shitty mood today. Maybe tomorrow will be better.

1.31.2019

I am so thankful to be healthy and have healthy children. God, please protect us. Things could be so much worse. Forgive me if I am ungrateful, Lord, for I know I am. The first month of the year has been conquered, or at the very least, I survived.

february

2019

Currently

MAKING myself better

LOVING every new day

WATCHING That 70s Show

WANTING to be toned and happy

READING nothing. but I checked out books

LISTENING to my children play

EATING right for the first time in a long time

DRINKING water but not nearly enough

HATING my temper

THINKING I matter

PLANNING my short story

WISHING we didn't have to struggle

2.1.2019

I've had a terrible, stressful morning. I tried to leave on time to take Miyah to her ultrasound. I had to take the younger two as well, and it's one of the coldest days of the year. The passenger door would not open; maybe it's frozen shut. The girls had to shuffle through the front of the car, and I had to drag the infant car seat as well. I forgot the prescription for the doctor and had to wait for it to be faxed over.

Despite the door not opening properly, one of the *other* doors wasn't closed all the way, and for my sanity, I couldn't figure out which one. The car beeped incessantly the entire time we were out.

2.2.2019

I haven't done the best on my diet this week, but I still feel good about myself. I have been pushing myself to accomplish quite a few goals at one time, and I know if I keep on, I will really achieve them.

Miyah had her first father-daughter dance. Irshaad also took Angel, and they both looked beautiful. I took pictures before they left, and all three of them posed all silly and cool, like they were doing glamour shots with friends at the mall! I need to start the kids' scrapbooks this year. I've been collecting things for years, even for Q.

So I got a day to myself pretty much. The baby slept while the girls were gone. I did a facial, showered, worked on my planner, and started to retwist my locs. It was almost a perfect day alone. I need more days like this. They are good for my brain.

2.3.2019

Super Bowl Sunday. Made cake from scratch; it was just OK, a bit dry if I'm being honest. The halftime show was terrible. The game was *so* boring, but I had a great night with friends. Ate like shit all weekend; however, I have my meal preps waiting for me this week in the fridge.

2.4.2019

I officially feel like I've hit a wall. I don't feel like finishing my foreword. I want to eat junk. I want to sleep. I want to shop endlessly. I have set goals for this month, the week, and each day, and it's starting to feel like too much. But I know that doesn't mean I should just stop now. I lost seven pounds last month. I got back into my writing group; I'm going to be in an anthology. I'm getting to where I want to be, but getting there and staying there are two different things.

2.5.2019

So I did morning yoga and meditation. I have been eating right and did my intense ab workout. And ... I was feeling like a cranky, bitchy mother. I was shamelessly careless. My children were not in any harm or anything, but I honestly felt detached.

Well, I just woke up from a nap, a badly needed nap, and I feel refreshed. I never let myself nap with the kids because I always feel like I have something else I need to get done. And even now, I have a few things on my to-do list to complete, hopefully before Miyah gets home. But I feel so much better. Getting rest is self-care, too.

2.6.2019

Today is better. A lot better. Almost done with my foreword. Sore from working out, and baby Aaliyah is five months old today. I am going to sleep.

2.7.2019

Every time I think about where my writing is, I feel hopeful and overwhelmed. I have so many projects in the works, most of them still in my head. I want my words to be shared so badly, but then I wonder how they will be received. I wish I could say I was thick-skinned, but I am not. I am sensitive AF. I desperately want the approval of others. I am striving to not care so much, but it's hard. I try way too hard, in a way that's so obvious and desperate, you can smell it a mile away.

2.8.2019

My husband's pain is my pain. I don't know how he still moves so effortlessly and stands so tall and confident. I cry when he tells me stories. I also laugh and cringe at some of his anecdotes. My husband is the epitome of a strong black man. Sometimes I don't feel like I deserve him, like I'm not strong enough to stand beside him, much less behind him. I pray the day comes when he no longer has to prove himself and his worth. I yearn for the time people treat him as well as he treats them. I am waiting for my husband to get what he *deserves*.

2.9.2019

Self-Care Saturday! So I did a facial and went out by myself to buy a few things for my kitchen. Of course, I ended up buying the girls, Q, and Irshaad things they don't need for Valentine's Day. I don't know why I do it, but it feels good to buy them things, even if I'm supposed to be buying for myself. This time I did. I'm about to watch a movie and spend time with my husband. All the kids are finally in bed.

2.10.2019

One of the busiest and most insane Sundays ever. I'm completely exhausted, and there are a handful of chores waiting for me in the morning.

I'm struggling a bit right now with my anxiety. It always presents itself in different ways. For the past six months or so, it's been the little voice in my head telling me I won't be able to properly swallow my food and will choke. It sucks. So much. Also, happy thirtieth birthday, Ricky!

2.11.2019

Finally started working on what I think will be the final edit for my essay that's being published! I feel kind of vulnerable sharing this with the world. The essay is about my anxiety and how it has affected me. I talk about my irrational thoughts, which fuel my panic attacks. I have overcome the—let's be honest—embarrassing aspect that accompanies my panic attacks, and I have been open about it. I still feel like it's hard for others to empathize; I feel like my own sister just doesn't get it (or care). Maybe things will be different after the essay comes out. Notice how I care so much.

2.12.2019

So I've been doing meatless dinners and days to help me lose some weight. So far, I've had loaded quesadillas enough times to be sick of them. I also had BBQ cauliflower bites for dinner last night. They were … OK, and I love BBQ sauce, but I don't think I will be eating that again unless I can find another recipe. There is a learning curve to this healthy food meal prep. I've made some pretty gross things. Cookies made with bananas, oatmeal, and chocolate chips sounded good, but the smell of cooked banana made Miyah *gag*, and I felt queasy after eating it. I have a pretty good routine of what I eat on a daily. But I want yummy things, too.

2.13.2019

Irshaad came home early because of the snow, and I'm so happy. I have quite a few items on my to-do list that need to get done. I've been talking with BB about how overwhelming these 2019 goals have become. So far, the only thing I have been able to commit to the most is eating better. I haven't even done yoga or meditation lately. I still haven't done my vision board. My writing habits are better, though. My mentor hooked me up with a writing buddy, and I think we're going to be great writing friends.

2.14.2019

2019 goals, who? Tell that to the empty bag (OK, two empty bags) of Lindt chocolate truffles. Tell that to my biceps; we hardly knew ya. Tell that to my yoga mat collecting dust in a corner. Well, there is always Monday to start again. Happy Valentine's Day.

2.15.2019

In, like, two days I think I have dismantled all the hard work I have been putting in. To punish myself, I have binged on so many calories; I will probably be digesting this shit for days. In other news, I'm thinking of making and selling some

African print jewelry. I need to start off by buying some fabric and materials. I really want to contribute some income to this household. I hate that the world is on Irshaad's shoulders.

2.16.2019

Today was the sixth day in a row of being in the house with the kids until Irshaad came home, and it showed. Mean, cranky mommy was here. I did a little self-care with a facial, but I was miserable. I was ready to run out (to food shop) as soon as Irshaad got home, but I ended up not going. Instead, I laid up with my husband and binge-watched Netflix. It felt nice.

2.17.2019

I decided to make some all-natural house cleaners. I finally bought the supplies and made them today. I decided to look up some home remedies for this cold I have, but after swallowing a tablespoon of honey, I promptly threw up all my dinner. I went to a yoga class today. I enjoyed it. My mat was ugly and worn, my pants were frayed a bit on one of the designs, and I was quite uncoordinated, but I enjoyed it. I'm making Sunday yoga workouts *outside* of the house a habit. Namaste.

2.18.2019

Thinking about trying the women's five-dollar workout class on Sundays. I'm nervous, but I think it might be good for me to get out of the house and get into a workout class with other humans.

2.19.2019

I definitely feel like I am not giving Angel, my middle child, enough attention. She's home with me during the day, but I don't engage with her enough. She wears her sister's hand-me-downs and rarely gets anything new. Lately, I have tried to make a point to play little games with her during the day and read to her, but I always tell her to wait when she wants my attention or wants to do something. I never feel like getting down to play with her. I'm always busy trying to get my own chores done or work out. I'm always telling her "I have to get the baby" when she's trying to hug me for a long time. It's not OK, especially because I am someone who craves affection as well. I need to do better by my Angel.

2.20.2019

I hate drama because I hate having to be confrontational. It honestly makes me so uncomfortable. But it's necessary.

2.21.2019

There really needs to be more greenery in my house. I want more life in this house. I want to be a plant mom.

2.22.2019

I've already let my self-doubt come in and make me question my goals. That little voice in my head is judging me for wanting to do things outside the norm. That little voice keeps saying, "What will they think?" I always feel like if I just go for what I want and really push myself, my greatness is within my reach. My calling and my time are here, and I'm scared to let myself out there. Stop the madness, Dana. Stop the fucking madness.

2.23.2019

Another long week has come to a close. I'm going out to the movies with my ladies tonight. I really need some me-time. All week, I have been doing this seven-day workout challenge, along with eating very clean (except the Chinese I had for dinner). It claims to help you lose one to two inches from your waist. I will see if I have any worthy results on Monday. My stomach is the real problem. It's just so big and loose and ugly, and it feels so foreign to me, like it's not mine. Even with the scale tipping, my good habits feel futile if I don't actually see results. I can't stop what I'm doing. I want to look good naked.

2.24.2019

I feel incredible. BB and I went to that workout class this morning. Then, we shopped a little, and I went home and spent the rest of the day with my family. The class was great. I finished my seven-day workout, and I measured myself again. I lost *inches* in my belly! It feels so good to do the things I said I would. I've never been this dedicated to actually losing weight before, not even for my wedding. And now, BB and I have a Sunday ritual. I would prefer to stay home on Sundays, but it's literally the only day I can get out right now.

2.25.2019

My sister and niece are coming to visit in two weeks, and I'm excited to spend time with them. It's been a year-and-a-half since I've seen Drea and Cruz; I miss them so much. I always call Drea my twin; we were both born in May—me the sixth, her the seventh—but I'm three years older. You wouldn't know it, though, because I get bossed around by her a lot. Out of all of my siblings, she's the most aggressive, the most confident, and the most effortlessly cool. She is my best friend, and she finally ditched that loser boyfriend. #Growth

2.26.2019

Irshaad is working the overnight shift, and it fucking sucks. Granted, I can now use my car during the day if I need to, so that's good, but once he leaves for work at 2:45 p.m., it's a wrap. He hates it. It's fucking freezing outside, and it's already fucking with his sleep. He's been sleeping on the couch because our queen bed just isn't big enough with the baby, so now I'm sequestered in the room, trying to keep quiet until noon, which is cramping my style. My husband's work never serves a happy medium; either they sit him and we're broke as shit, relying on unemployment, or he's worked to the bone, and to be honest, his morale drops and so does mine. February is almost over. Tax money is coming soon.

Dana Muwwakkil

2.27.2019

I was feeling low all day, and I can correlate the feeling to eating like shit again. I ended up taking an unofficial cheat day with foods I don't even really like. It started with my morning coffee being *way* too sweet and just ballooned from there. Our tax money came, and I've been doing some online virtual shopping, but I can't wait to get out and get some things on my own. I bought some workout leggings. They only had XL and medium. I've been in XL for a long time, but I bought medium and tried them on earlier, and they actually kind of … fit? I still haven't donned my old jeans yet, and I have a feeling they won't be as forgiving, especially on my little pooch.

2.28.2019

So I'm having a stressful and anxiety-inducing morning. I need to not lean on shit food to comfort me. I will update later. Hopefully, victoriously …

I ate like crap the rest of the day but mostly out of convenience and temptation. I had yogurt before I went shopping with BB. I came home starving, and Irshaad was eating tortilla chips with melted cheese—my kryptonite. It was good. No regrets.

march

2019

Currently

LOVING Chobani Flip yogurt

MAKING some strides and some baby steps

READING Whispers and Roars

THINKING about redecorating

EATING quite well

WISHING I didn't have to wish for anything

HATING how quickly I rationalize to avoid confrontation

PLANNING on losing this jiggly belly

DRINKING water as usual

WANTING to see my husband more

3.1.2019

Hello, March. I went to the eye doctor today, and I reinvented myself, if only for the appointment. I played the part of a smiley extrovert. I think I did a good job. My eye doc is a great guy, the staff was nice, and the office was cute and cozy (besides the creepy painted child's portrait in the lobby). In that office, I was the confident, relaxed person I wish I was everywhere I go.

3.2.2019

Drove for an hour to the Danbury mall and spent most of our money on the girls. They had a great time. Miyah was so indecisive at the Disney Store but eventually settled on a Belle Barbie and Beast. Angel immediately picked up a Princess Tiana and Prince Naveen set. For different reasons, I'm proud of both of their choices. I don't usually allow white Barbies or dolls in my house, but for Belle, I make the exception. I ate a sandwich before we left and only had a soda and ice cream when we were out because I didn't want to deal with the agonizing situation of trying to eat in a crowded food court, somehow convinced the food I'm trying to swallow will get stuck in my throat, causing me to choke. I have got to get my ass to my psychiatrist.

3.3.2019

Miyah's belly started hurting her again. She stopped complaining of pains for about two weeks, and I hoped whatever she had passed. It didn't. I hate seeing my daughter in pain. We've been tracking her foods but have no clue what could be triggering the pain.

My period feels like it's coming every day, and I'm slightly freaked out that it hasn't arrived yet. It came around the seventh of January, and I didn't track in February. I can't have any more kids after the tubal ligation that almost killed me, but I am terrified of having an ectopic pregnancy. I'm also still traumatized by that event. Women can't win when it comes to birth control. My last child's birth has fucked me up both physically and mentally.

3.4.2019

So hype! One of my poems was accepted into a local talent art gallery thing! The judges chose thirty poems, and there are eighteen artists. It's up to the artist to choose a poem they like and reinterpret it in any artistic way they choose. I'm so giddy and nervous. Validation like this makes me feel like a good writer. I hope my poem is chosen by one of the artists. There is also a ceremony and an opening night, and I can read my poem if I want! Ah, I'm already reading it out loud … but I hate the way my voice sounds. Ugh. Self-doubt is a bitch, but I am going to practice my power poses and my speaking voice in the mirror.

3.5.2019

Finished *We're Going to Need More Wine* by Gabrielle Union. Pretty good memoir.

3.6.2019

I can't believe I had Aaliyah exactly six months ago.

3.7.2019

Grouchy, sad, tired, want-a-fucking-break mommy is back. The "no" and "get out" mommy is back. The "no matter how hard I try, no one gives a fuck" mommy is back. The "I can't put a dent in the dishes," "the laundry never ends" mommy is back. The "screaming for help" mommy is back. The "I don't care" mommy is back.

3.8.2019

I didn't work out today. I ate an entire sleeve of Oreos for no reason today. Tomorrow will be better. I'll get back on my shit tomorrow.

3.9.2019

I finally got my mom on the phone. I haven't had a real conversation with her in a long time. I haven't even told her that I lost this weight. I tried to video chat, but she couldn't hear me, so we talked on the phone, but she was babysitting, and we kept getting interrupted. It hurt. I broke down crying and said into the phone, "I never get to talk to you." My mom apologized and promised to do better. I'm trying to decide if I should work out … or wash Angel's hair … or wash the dishes … or just do nothing. If I do nothing, all those things will grow legs and multiply.

3.10.2019

Mom called me this morning, and we spoke for almost an hour.

3.11.2019

I got a new laptop today. So far, the keyboard feels very foreign to me, and I don't like that aspect, but I know I will settle in. I'm off to start some new writing. Five days till Drea's arrival.

3.12.2019

An OK day.

3.13.2019

Cleaning like mad so another family member doesn't comment on how "shitty" or "dirty" my house is when Drea gets here. I sobbed like a baby when I was in the hospital after just giving birth (and almost dying) and Irshaad told me when he went home to check on my dad and the kids, my dad seemed a lot more concerned with my role as a housewife and mother than anything else. Hey, guys, I never said I was June fucking Cleaver. If they only knew how much time I spend just trying to maintain some order through all this chaos. If anyone ever knew how hard it is to be a stay-at-home mom. I started eating like crap again, but I'm still working out. Right now, maintaining where I am is ideal. Well, OK, I'm lying. I would love to lose more weight, but my eating doesn't reflect that.

3.14.2019

Tomorrow is supposed to be a big deal. Other than the fact that my family is coming in, I'm looking forward to seeing if my poem was chosen by any artist for the showcase I'm in. I have a one-in-two shot they will choose mine. Of course, I'm banking on not getting selected because that's just how I am. Negative. I'm trying to make my presence on social media bigger so when I actually put my own book out and my other bookmark project, I have a bit of an audience already. Unfortunately, I'm moving at a snail's pace with getting my following bigger. I'm just not cool. I don't say that to be down on myself, but I feel like, even with social media, everything is a popularity contest. And it doesn't matter what sort of tribe or subgenre you enter, either; there is always a caste system.

3.15.2019

My sister and niece are here, and they brought gorgeous weather with them. The day is warm and long. My husband's car is out of the shop, so I have complete access to my vehicle again. Irshaad also finally stopped working nights, which is a blessing. The house looks great and feels good. I have time this evening to read, write, and work out. I am happy. I never got an email saying my poem was chosen, although every time I saw I had mail waiting in my inbox, my heart fluttered. I keep telling myself it doesn't matter if some artists liked my poem or not, but honestly, I really wanted the validation from another creative. I thought the collaboration would be dope to see. I can't say I'm not disappointed.

3.16.2019

We went to one of our couple friends' houses today and had dinner with them and hung out. They are a young black couple with a very sweet and funny ten-year-old daughter, a cute and shy two-year-old son, and a gorgeous home. I haven't seen them in a while, and it took me a bit to come out of my shell again. I kept getting tongue-tied and losing my train of thought and sounding moronic. There were times when I observed everyone else, just playing and laughing and joking, and it was so effortless. I want to connect on that level so badly, but I can't. I can if it's one-on-one or if I'm super comfortable, but it takes me a long time to get super comfortable. I'm always the one on the outside smiling nervously because I don't know what else to do, always thinking about what I should say minutes before I say it. And I'm always worried someone will see me pretending to be normal.

3.17.2019

BB couldn't make our workout class, so I went alone. I came home and rushed to get the girls ready so we could all drive to Bounce together for Cruz's birthday party that was put together by Drea's best friend's parents. My sister is so lucky; she has a tribe everywhere she goes, a support system on this coast and where she lives in Vegas. I'm envious of that. I wish

Irshaad and I had someone to help us with our children, take them for a Saturday afternoon, a weekend here and there. But it is what it is. The party itself was so nice, but I was uncomfortable. The place was crowded as hell, and all of my sisters' friends kept trying to talk and catch up with me, and I just stuttered my way through conversations, hating myself the entire time. *Dana, why are you like this?* Drea has spent the first two nights at her best friend's parents' house; I'm worried I won't really get to see her during this trip. It hurts my feelings.

3.18.2019

I feel like the world's worst mother today. Miyah and Q were at school, and I wanted to go to this discount store to get Aaliyah and Miyah some packs of socks and do a little shopping for myself. As I was loading the car, I realized I forgot something and went back to the house. As I was approaching the stairs to get back inside, Miyah's bus dropped her off; she'd had a half-day. Not only did my sister witness this shocking event, but I couldn't stop thinking about what would have happened if I hadn't been held up. What if I wasn't there for Miyah when she got off that bus? What if the driver let her off and she came home to an empty house? What if she wasn't allowed off the bus and was left wondering where her mother was? I had a flashback of when I had Girl Scouts in fourth grade. After the meeting, in the evening, I waited by the door to the school for my mom's car, but she never came. After panicking silently for fifteen minutes while everyone else got picked up, my troop leader, who finally noticed me pacing at the door, finally said, "Oh, Dana, your mom asked me to take you home."

3.19.2019

Yesterday was Cruz's sixth birthday. I blew up some balloons and bought a giant "6" balloon for her. She was a bit unimpressed by my efforts. We spent the last four days celebrating her birthday already, so I don't blame her. At just six years old, my niece is more well-traveled than my thirty-year-old husband. That's going to change soon. We booked two vacations for the summer, baby! The Jersey shore in Seaside Heights and Hershey Park in Pennsylvania. Not nearly as cool as Disney World but baby steps for me. I'm excited as hell. This will be our first family vacation ever.

3.20.2019

I missed my alarm this morning. I woke up at 8:30 a.m., with Miyah missing her bus. What is going on with me this week? I figured I would have Drea look after Angel and the baby while I ran Miyah to school, but nobody was here. Drea went to a museum in the city with Cruz. The day went on for me like any other day, besides me not working out and me eating like a pig for no reason. I ate so much junk today, my stomach hurt. I will finally see my brother tomorrow. I haven't seen him since last May, and he only lives forty-five minutes away. My family is so weird. We are close but distant. Scattered all over but bonded. So the only person to not meet Aaliyah on my side will be my mom. Who knows when she will?

3.21.2019

At the last minute, Drea and I discovered a show to binge-watch before she leaves. We always bond over movies and television. We had a few movie nights planned while she was here, but we never had a chance to actually watch them. It's great seeing my brother Ricky. Unfortunately, he was not able to conceal his still-present struggle with alcohol. I hope he gets help soon because I want him to be happy, truly happy, but he's still in the denial stage. My last night with Drea and Cruz was a good one. Farewell, my siblings.

3.22.2019

My sister and brother left for Florida this morning. They are flying to see my dad and visit Disney World. My dad invited my family to go as well and was willing to pay for us. I declined. I said the baby was too young. I said I wasn't ready for a trip like that yet. I said I didn't want to go to Disney World just because my dad thinks it's time, and all of this is true, but there is more to it. For one, I'm terrified of flying. I haven't flown in over ten years because, the truth is, I'm a lot worse now than I was then. That's not all of it, either. There is something about my anxiety that is almost like agoraphobia; the farther I am away from my home, the more uneasy I feel, the more I feel I'm going to die. So that's why I declined the trip this year. That's why we're going to do Hershey Park and Seaside. Baby steps.

3.23.2019

Last night was exciting and scary and uncomfortable. We went to the gallery my poem was featured in for the opening ceremony. Part of a strip mall, the place was pretty tiny and packed with other poets and artists. It was the perfect opportunity to network and speak to other people in my field. Naturally, I hid behind my children and was wrangled into a few conversations my husband (who swears he's an introvert) was having. All my awkwardness aside, I'm so proud of myself. After that, we went to eat delicious burgers at Red Robin. I sucked down my root beer float and took tiny bites of my mouth-watering bacon cheeseburger. I cut my burger in half and ate half of the half and swirled around my fries. The fear of choking was too great. I couldn't wait to get home to my safety net so I could actually eat my food, which I am doing now. Going to watch a movie with my supportive husband and probably bone. Goodnight.

3.24.2019

I decided to take the girls to story time at the library. I took too long to start getting them ready. I ended up yelling and stressing while getting them dressed and clean, all the while feeling like such a mean mom and wondering why I was even taking them if it caused that much stress. Of course, we still went to the library. When story time was over, I ordered a new book and picked up one to read in the meantime. Laundry later.

3.25.2019

I hopped right back into my old routine like I never left. I'm still craving the junk foods I was eating this past week, but I handled myself well. I also made dental appointments for the entire family and brought my planner back out. It really helps keep me on track. I'm feeling less motivated when it comes to my own book of poetry and essays I hope to self-publish this year. For one, it's not going to be cheap, and for another, it's going to be hard work. I have done one draft on one essay, and while editing it, I found myself so overwhelmed. Being a lazy writer has been my calling for so long; it's what I do best. It's almost April, and I am still dreaming of being great.

3.26.2019

The husband is going to be home for a while. Honestly, I'm not sure how long because things change in his line of work so suddenly. We can't live off of unemployment, but we have enough saved up from our tax money to provide a cushion for a little while, so I'm going to enjoy Irshaad being home each day. I already feel the stress from running the house coming off my shoulders. I have gotten a lot of my tasks done today but have saved working on my current writing project for last. My editor for my published essay contacted me with the final edits, and although my essay has changed quite a bit since its conception, I am quite happy with it. I need to work on my bio and am having a hard time coming up with something witty and engaging. I also need to take a few new pictures to go with my profile. Ah, the life of a writer. Hey, I'm happy today.

3.27.2019

Dad's birthday. I waited until Miyah got home from school, and all the girls and I sang "Happy Birthday" to him when he picked up. I sent my dad the info about my poem, and he asked how I did at the gallery opening. I recently told him about my article as well, and it was weird because although writing is such a huge part of my life, I never share it with my dad. I always feel like there is this elephant in the room. When I was in eighth grade, I wrote a very raw poem about my feelings for my father, and he found it. I told him I had written the poem based on something I had read, and he said he believed me. But maybe he only wanted to. I drafted an essay about our tumultuous relationship, but it was more therapeutic than anything. Our relationship is better than it's ever been now, and my father and I have spoken about our past. He's even acknowledged and apologized for his behavior, which really helped, and I appreciate it. But how he treated me during that time helped shape me into who I am today, for better or for worse. It's my truth, but I don't want to hurt my dad.

Dana Muwwakkil

3.28.2019

I did an insane workout today, and I killed it! I ate like a champ. I went to the library for two blissful hours to work on my writing and enjoy my own thoughts. So why was I such a mean bitch to my children today? I wanted to take them outside, but Irshaad decided to go weld, so I opted to take them with me to the store. I just didn't have any patience left in me. And the terrible part is I really have no excuse for how mean and impatient I was. Sometimes I really think I am becoming my father. I don't yell as much, but I can say hurtful things when I'm tired or frustrated or overwhelmed. God, don't let them hate me.

3.29.2019

Today, I took a cheat day. I never plan my cheat days; they just sort of happen. We went food shopping, and I got all my healthy foods: turkey burgers, pita bread, my favorite yogurts. Then, I came home and had a yummy sandwich and added a bit of bacon as a treat. Then, I binged on graham crackers. I could feel my stomach stretching out and screaming, "Bitch, what is you doin'?" I'm not going to beat myself up over it anymore. I am still great. I'm actually still sore from yesterday's workout, a soreness that tells me I'm doing something.

3.30.2019

Gorgeous day today. Just realized March wasn't as shitty as I anticipated, no snow. I'm going out tonight, so I'm looking forward to that. I took the girls to run around in the yard, and they were bursting with excitement. Baby Aaliyah was just fascinated to be out there, looking at the big, beautiful world. I look at her and can't believe she is really mine. She is so big now and trying hard to keep up with her big sisters.

3.31.2019

Last night, I went to the movies with my friend. We are slowly building our friendship. We were brought together by our husbands. We had a great time, and the movie was so damn good and creepy. Jordan Peele (the writer and director) is one of my heroes right now. His writing is funny, engaging, and thoughtful. I have always been into film and lowkey want to write a screenplay. The night wasn't perfect, I will admit. A young woman about my age tested me at the movies by shining her bright-ass phone around in a dark theater while arriving late. Her phone landed and stayed on my face for a few seconds, and I made a "What the fuck?" gesture. Then, this same woman and her friend ended up next to my friend and me, and at the climax of the film, she pulled out her bright-ass phone and got on Facebook. I obviously looked in her direction, trying to prompt her to stop, but she didn't give a fuck. Both of her disruptions caused me to miss integral parts.

When I got home, I felt bad for not speaking up. Her actions were wrong and a distraction. This is the second time this month a young black woman like myself has done some bullshit in my vicinity, and I chose to act passively. I think I'm afraid of my saying something turning the situation into a fight. I don't want to fight with anybody, and these days, people are quick to film something and upload it. So should I just keep my mouth shut and be taken for a ride, or should I say something and maybe get into a fight?

april

2019

Currently

LOVING the longer days

MAKING a reason for being

READING Don't Touch My Hair

THINKING I used the dumbest senior quote in 2008

WISHING Don't we all wish to be rich?

HATING how unsure I can be

PLANNING my book

DRINKING water, water, and more water

WANTING more alone time

4.1.2019

It is National Poetry Month. My sister (close friend, Amanda), who is also an author/poet, challenged me (and, well, anyone) to write a poem a day all month. Maybe one or two will be halfway decent. Maybe I can finish a few I started and abandoned. Here is today's poem

> *Why won't you say you love me*
> *when we say goodbye?*
> *Why don't you say you trust me,*
> *then look me in my eye?*

4.2.2019

> *A trash man*
> *is a trash man,*
> *and I ain't talking 'bout the trash, man.*

This is the second week of Irshaad being home, and we know the drill. He has filed for unemployment, and we have to wait a week before he gets paid. I am so thankful we (meaning him) decided to save as much money as we did because the unemployment is only going to cover our bills for the month and not our rent. I wish I had bought everyone's Easter stuff already and the things I wanted to get Q for his birthday. I have been eyeing a Steelers bedspread, and I wanted to totally redo his room. And he requested some Nike shorts, so an outfit would be around eighty bucks if we do that. I still have my payment for my essay that could help cover those above-mentioned expenses, but I have many plans for that money. I guess we shall see.

4.3.2019

I'm tired. I recently came to the realization that I will not be able to get my writing done for my own project (my love child book) if I don't *make* the time. I put writing dead last. I've even thrown in reading, working on Instagram posts (it's working; my followers are growing), and anything else in front of my writing! Working out, cleaning, and other things have me busy. When I finally crash, I crash. Oh, yeah; I'm not doing a poem a day anymore. Easy come, easy go.

4.4.2019

So it's before six a.m. (thanks, Aaliyah), and I just decided I'm going to put the coffee on and try to get some writing done right now while Aaliyah watches a show that keeps her entertained. Usually, I use this time to catch a few extra winks while I can, but let's see what happens.

I really need help. My anxiety is raging. I took Miyah to see the gastro this morning. I have been dreading the trip for weeks because the drive to get to the doctor's office has a scary merge onto this weird highway, which I fucking hate, and you merge from the right, not the left. In the hours leading up to us leaving, I was stressing so badly, and when I'm stressed, I am completely terrible. Miyah had nothing but questions and wouldn't stop squealing with excitement and enthusiasm, and it just made it worse. I had to send her out of my room several times (because she kept coming back). Before I made it to the scary part of the trip, I had to stop at the toll booth. It's usually quick, but there was a wait today that made my anxiety ten times worse. I wanted to just turn around and go home, but I couldn't. I kept thinking about how Miyah needs to get help. Then, we went to Wendy's, and I just sat there, staring at my delicious food. I was too afraid to eat. I am exhausted from the physical stress of it all. Will this never end?

4.5.2019

I got off the phone with my dad in near tears. It was a good thing. I had an open and honest discussion with him about my mental health and told him I need help right now, and he told me he understood. He wasn't judgmental or hurtful. It means so much to have my father's support. I made an appointment to see my therapist today. I also fit into my favorite pair of Levi's that I haven't worn in around two years.

4.6.2019

Aaliyah is seven months today. I'm in the parking lot of the laundromat. It's gorgeous outside, and I'm sitting in my car trying to read my book, but I can't relax. Cars keep coming in and out, I keep thinking I'm going to let my dryer expire, and I'm worried about bleeding through my clothes (my period said, "Hey, I'm Beetlejuice, and it's showtime!"). Why can't I just chill? I'm going to run some errands after I do the laundry, and I won't have any more alone time until tomorrow's workout class. Get a grip, Dana.

4.7.2019

I didn't go to my workout class today, and BB told me it was Beyoncé Day, just my damn luck. My period is becoming a liability, and I didn't want to chance it. I'm buying the cup before my next period. As far as my weight loss journey goes, I took some photos this week, and just comparing them to the ones I took maybe a week before Drea came, I look so much better! Leaner, toned, my legs have slimmed, and there isn't as much cellulite. I even put on my "skinny" jeans the other day. But my stomach. It has shrunk considerably, but it's still ugly and embarrassing. I swear I would be perfectly happy if it looked the way it did before my pregnancy. It's saggy still. I'm terrified it won't go away, no matter what I do. I have a sneaking suspicion that maybe cutting out added sugar for a week or two will really help, but I'm not strong enough! I guess I don't want it badly enough. Mom is seven months sober.

4.8.2019

Irshaad took all three of the girls outside so I could relax for a while in the house with some quiet. After I was done messaging BB, taking a shower, and reading my book for all of ten minutes, Irshaad brought the baby back in as she whined, saying she had had enough. She was really the one I wanted a break from. I just had to come to the realization that it will be a long time until I can expect to stretch out on my own bed and relax without an infant tugging at my shirt or wanting me to pick her up and play.

4.9.2019

I woke up with a killer headache and did my usual remedies of medicine, coffee, and a hot shower, and it finally went away. My anxiety is fucking with me badly. Lately, I've been looking online, trying to figure out what I am going to go to school for, and it's so overwhelming. For the longest time, I wanted to do the medical assistant program. It's six months long, the job prospects are plentiful, and the pay is decent. There is one program over here, but there is no financial aid available. I think my dad would help me pay for it. I'm also very interested in a drug and alcohol counselor program. It could be six months to a year long with financial aid, but I wasn't too thrilled about the job listings I've seen. I've also been considering just getting my associates in human services. Working with people and helping them is one of my aspirations in life. So, do I want the long term or short term? Will I be fulfilled with any of these options?

And also, as much as I hate being home alone with my children, I love and am lucky that I can be here for them. My children don't have to be in daycare. They are with their mama, their nurturer. I'm not ready to leave them. Ideally, I could work from home. Ideally, I could stay home until my children are all in school.

4.10.2019

I went to the library to write. I spent most of my time writing and rewriting a terrible scene in a work of fantasy/science fiction that's been in my head. Do writers often cross from nonfiction to fiction? Although most of my published work is nonfiction, I've completed more fiction projects than anything else thus far. I've written two novels that will probably never see the light of day and a ton of stories I've started but couldn't finish.

I caught up on my reading while I was at the library, so that was nice. So happy to be reading and getting lost in a book. Like with writing, I had to make time for it to make it work.

4.11.2019

A little update on my fitness goals: I'm still working out about five days a week. I'm still eating clean for the most part. My arms have actual muscle, and I need to move up to heavier weights. I might buy some next time we go to Walmart. My back looks great, too, but I want to be more toned in both areas and for it to be more obvious. I'm so happy I have stuck with these changes for four months. I have changed part of my life. And I'm happy.

4.12.2019

I'm sick,
though you can't see it.
It never goes away,
and it's a bitch to treat it.
Some empathize,
most don't believe it.
This ain't a fable,
and I have no sword to beat it.

4.13.2019

There is a poetry fest next Saturday, and I want to go, but I'm
scared. I'm such an insecure person. I feel like I will be singled
out for not belonging there, that people will be able to read the
discomfort on my face, which is always present when I'm in
social situations. I could go and bring my children and husband,
but then I will be hiding behind them the whole time. I could go
alone and be terribly awkward, too, instead of meeting people
and making connections. It's an annual thing, so I keep telling
myself I'll go next year, that I will be the better, more confident
version of myself next year. Here's to being a coward. Again.

4.14.2019

I went to my workout class this morning, and only three other
ladies showed up, so the class was very intimate, to say the
least. I couldn't blend into the background like I'm used to. I
worked on making eye contact with our instructor because

I've realized I have a thing with looking people in the eye. It makes me extremely uncomfortable. I have a writer's meeting tonight, and I'm a little bit nervous because I submitted a deeply personal essay about my mental state called "Does That Make Me Crazy?" I hope they like it, but I'm also worried they won't find my essay relatable. Will they think I'm crazy? More importantly, am I?

4.15.2019

I went to the library and did my first round of submissions for this year. I submitted my poetry to three sites. I'm trying to figure out if I really want to do this anymore. In the last two years, I've submitted my work all over the place; do I still need the validation? I was listening to an interview with Toni Morrison, and she only had one short story published in a literary magazine her entire career. Obviously, I'm not Toni Morrison, but what am I getting out of this? Validation? I do have three publications I actually want to be featured in, but other than that, what is there for me? I've been reading nonfiction and memoirs like crazy, and I'm really enjoying it. My fellow writers from my writing group all enjoyed my personal essay. I think I may be onto something if I can figure out what else to write for my own project.

4.16.2019

My husband finally got me the tulips I had been requesting for the last two or three years. Every time he would actually go to get them (my birthday or Mother's Day), they would be gone already. Men. He's been home for three weeks now, and I have my new routine down. I wake up early with Aaliyah, put on the coffee, and write. I get Miyah up for school, do her morning routine, and she goes on the bus. Then, I make breakfast for the baby, Angel, and me. I stay in my room reading or on the phone till around ten-ish. I wake Irshaad up so I can do my workouts without Aaliyah screaming, then I shower. A couple of times a week, I have been going to the library as well. I no longer feel that weight of our household (or loneliness or bitterness) on my shoulders. But as nice as this has been, hubby is starting to grow anxious because it's been so long since he's been called into work. And these are the times I wish I had an income, too, because he wouldn't have to stress at all, really. But I don't, so we are at his job's mercy.

4.17.2019

So my presence on social media is actually growing. Turns out, it's not as much of a popularity contest as I thought but more so about finding your niche. Mine is writing, poetry, and mental health. Posting hashtags helps a lot, too. Who knew? But now, I'm wondering if this is what I really want to do. Most of my time has been focused on picking the perfect picture, the right quote, and writing book reviews and thought-provoking captions. I am doing this to build my platform so when I do finally publish my book, I might have an actual following. But there is no guarantee. Already,

I have met so many people just like me, a lot of them with published projects I want to check out. It feels like a rat race, though. What is even the point because I have a sneaking suspicion I am going to be publishing this book for me, and it will go unnoticed and unread? And at this point, if I don't concentrate and hunker down, there won't even be a book.

4.18.2019

Took the baby to the doctor today, and I almost didn't even go. My anxiety was creeping up on me, telling me it's best not to leave the house. And I almost listened. I almost made up a lie that the office called and I had to reschedule. But I didn't. I did take the long way to get there, though. And I took the long way home. Regression. I used to do those things years ago when I was too afraid to take the highways, even locally.

4.19.2019

I am at the library, enjoying the quiet, and I keep looking at the clock on my laptop. This is the last day until who knows when that I can do this. Irshaad is going back to work on Monday. I'm happy, obviously. He needs to be working. I'm grateful, of course, because he has been home and has helped me tremendously for three whole weeks. I'm crushed that my routine has to change again. I got used to him being here for me, holding Aaliyah in his lap so I could work out, putting the girls to bed, cooking dinner, giving me time alone so I can have some peace. I needed this so badly. But the show must go on, right? I also came here to work on my other essays, but it's looking like that's just not happening right now.

4.20.2019

Been preparing for Easter tomorrow. We're going to our friends' house to celebrate. I remember one of the very first times we hung out with them, they invited us to come see a fight at their house, and I was nervous for weeks! Now, I'm mostly comfortable around them, and our kids are friends. I need time to warm up to people, but when I do, I feel free. I worked out today, but my heart wasn't really in it. Picking the right workouts is key for me, and I didn't. I also ate a ton of junk food all day. I'm going to eat like crap tomorrow as well, but I'm going to make sure I get in a good workout.

4.21.2019

Deviled eggs will be my kryptonite today. I don't want to stress today. I did a lot of prep yesterday, but I still don't know what I'm going to wear. I'm looking forward to having a great day. Hubby goes back to work tomorrow. :(

4.22.2019

Remember how I was saying I'm going to try and not be stressed? That was frickin' hilarious. Of course, I was stressed the hell out and mean and rigid up until we pulled out of the driveway. Of course, I was beating myself up for being so cold to my children. But I actually had a great day once we got to our friends' house. I love this friendship that is growing between Celina and me. I left feeling so happy. Irshaad is back to work today, and Miyah is back to school tomorrow. I'm feeling good and happy so far, and I have gotten most of my daily tasks taken care of today, including writing and working on a new essay. I hope this momentum stays with me.

4.23.2019

Second day at home with my tribe, and so far, so good. The baby let me get in a muscle-building workout. I've cleaned, and I'm chilling for a few minutes before I hop into the shower. Miyah and Q are back to school, and the two little ones are asleep. I keep anticipating Aaliyah waking up, so that's making it kind of hard to really relax, but I'm trying to force myself.

4.24.2019

Got the younger two dressed and fed by the time Miyah got on the bus, so we were able to run to Marshalls, Dollar Tree, and Walmart and get back home by 5:30. I picked a few last-minute gifts for Q's birthday tomorrow, did food shopping, and will be going back out tomorrow morning so Aaliyah can get her measles shot. I need to stay focused on my essay writing and reading. I'm not loving the book I have right now, so I'm having trouble really getting into it. I'm feeling very "meh" today about how my body is looking. Is my stomach really going down, or will I have a big ole belly forever? I mean, I did eat chocolate marshmallow bunnies from Easter a little while ago and had medium-sized fries from McDonald's, but damn, can I enjoy life?

4.25.2019

Q's birthday is today. I hope his day was special. I bought him balloons and the clothes he asked for, and I made two batches of brownies. We love you, Q. Man. I remember when I was fourteen; my priorities were very much that of a teenager: fun, friends, boys, shopping, and movies. Sometimes I have to remind myself how teenagers think; it helps me understand my stepson a lot better.

4.26.2019

My destructive ways are so predictable and boring at this point, and I'm just over myself. I've eaten nothing but a ton of junk food bullshit, like so many calories worth of shit. I didn't have a real meal all day, just cheesecake, brownies, and fries. I'm in a funk from the shame, and I hate myself today. I have writing and house chores to catch up on. I don't feel like I'm in control right now. I did work out today, although it didn't put a dent in my calorie intake, but at least I did it. Eh, tomorrow will be better.

4.27.2019

Boring Saturday. My weighted gloves came in the mail (thanks, Amazon Prime), and I did my first kickboxing workout. I got to talk to my mama for a little while, and she's doing OK. Recovery is so damn hard. I'm so nervous about tomorrow; the poetry brunch is finally upon us. I've only started practicing my poem aloud *yesterday* because that's how I roll. I just don't want to stumble over my words. Irshaad has been laughing at me all night because he says my voice keeps changing. I just want to make sure everyone can hear me. I was telling him about when I ran to be secretary in the fourth grade Student Council. I wrote my own speech and thought I did a great job until a friend told me afterward that no one could hear me, even with the microphone.

4.28.2019

I read my poem in front of a packed crowd. I was calm in the moments leading up to my turn. We got there last, of course, so I was the last to speak, and I sat listening to the other poets and artists. But when it was my turn, I was so scared, and I never truly got lost in my poem. I kept having conscious thoughts while reading aloud. I kept thinking, *Make sure you're speaking into the mic; Look at the crowd; Don't hold your phone like that.* My best friend was there to support me, and my husband held Aaliyah in his arms for an hour because she wouldn't let him sit down. Irshaad also recorded me, and when I watched my playback, I wasn't cringing. It feels good to be pushed outside of my comfort zone. My mother-in-law watched the older two for us, so that helped with my stress level a lot. In all, this experience is something I can check off.

4.29.2019

I used to hate Mondays, but now, they are always a fail-safe for me to push myself to get back on track. I do well with my strength training and eat wholesome meals, then binge on my children's bullshit snacks. And once I start, I can't stop. I just ate my husband's little-ass Ding Dongs that I don't even really like, and they made my teeth hurt and piled on three hundred calories for no reason. I'm not even really satisfied.

4.30.2019

I went to have a consultation at the dentist today. They want to do surgery on my gums. It's so weird. I bought my mom a really dope Mother's Day card, and I can't wait to fill it out and send it to her. She's going to be so surprised. I also want to send one to my sister and BB and my other mommy friends. I need to get on that, though, because Mother's Day is the twelfth this year. My mom is having a rough time right now, and I want her to feel happy.

may

2019

Currently

LOVING that I conquered a fear of mine (public speaking)

MAKING progress with my latest personal essay

READING memoirs and nonfiction

THINKING about all the junk I need to get rid of

EATING curly fries. even though I meal- prepped a healthy soup

WISHING I knew what educational route to take

HATING this stubborn- ass mummy tummy

PLANNING a submission

DRINKING coffee

WANTING to really get my ass in gear

FEELING overwhelmed but not in a bad way

5.1.2019

It's May, the month I celebrate my birthday.

5.2.2019

I finally saw my therapist today. We had some catching up to do because it had been over a year since I last saw her. She thinks I'm doing better than when I first came to her, so she's happy about that, and we will see each other once a month to work on the techniques she's taught me. She OK'd my psych evaluation, so I'm going to see the psychiatrist in June and hopefully get back on my meds.

5.3.2019

One of those days. Don't feel like it.

5.4.2019

I gave myself a cheat day, although I haven't earned it. Hubby and I ate a massive dish of nachos with all the fixings and washed it down with soda. I also drank juice, which I never do, and ate more junk later. I know the next few days I won't be eating too well either, because I'm going to the movies tomorrow, and my birthday is Monday. I already bought my favorite, chocolate satin pie, to celebrate.

5.5.2019

Laundry day. I woke up at seven so I could go straight to the laundromat and get it done. Aaliyah's eyes popped open at the same exact time as mine, and I bundled her up and brought her with me. Everyone's clothes are drying now, and she is sleeping in her stroller. I have my workout class in a couple of hours, then Celina and I are going to see a movie in the afternoon.

5.6.2019

Today is my birthday. It was, in all, what it is for most people on their birthday: a regular-ass day. I did my usual. I worked out, played with the kids, went to the library, and got a new book (hopefully, a good one this time.) Irshaad got off work early and brought home yummy eats, then went to school. We ate chocolate silk pie. I wished for the same thing I wish for every year. I really feel like having a birthday a few months into the year, when New Year's resolutions have become fatigued, gives me a new sense of motivation to get my shit done. Being twenty-eight was OK; I'm looking forward to seeing what twenty-nine has in store for me.

5.7.2019

At the beginning of May, I said I was overwhelmed but in a good way. Well, that's a load of hogwash! I have so many little things in the corner of my mind stressing me out. Everywhere I turn, I see clutter, something that needs to be replaced or put away. The girls' winter and fall clothes need to be sorted and organized into the attic. Aaliyah's baby clothes need to be archived and bagged. My closet spills with junk every time I open one of the doors. Baseboards and doors need to be scrubbed. My hair needs to be washed and twisted. Everyone needs new curtains, and mail needs to be sorted. I have so many writing tasks. My planner is unorganized. All I have right now is a good book to keep me somewhat sane while the older girls bathe and Aaliyah sleeps.

5.8.2019

I have finally decided what I am going to school for. I am going to go to my local SUNY and get my associates in human services! At the end of the day, this is a field I am most passionate about (other than writing), and I am excited to start this road to a new career.

5.9.2019

I applied to school online, and the process was very simple. Two steps to go: have my official transcripts sent and take the placement tests. I know I need to study for the math portion because I have done this before, just never finished my education. Hell, I didn't even finish a fucking semester. My anxiety was so bad, I stopped going to one of my classes, and I had trouble getting my work printed out for another class, and I was too afraid to ask for help. A problem with a USB drive caused enough stress for me to drop out of a class that I only half-paid for. I have reservations about being back in school and being around my peers again, being in an environment with people *everywhere* and me not knowing a soul. I can do this. I have to do this. It's time to take control of my life again.

5.10.2019

Today was great. First, I went to the dentist and had a silent panic attack while praying the numbing injection didn't send me into cardiac arrest. After about ten minutes, when I realized I was OK, I was able to relax. As a treat afterward, I went to Barnes & Noble. I don't think I've been there during a weekday, and it was so nice and quiet. I spent my time looking at journals, knickknacks, and cookbooks. After browsing for about an hour, I sat down with a delicious cafe mocha and did some freestyle writing and thinking. I left refreshed. At home, we watched *Jumanji* with the girls. Angel wanted to watch it again immediately after it ended, and Miyah vowed to never watch it again because it was "too scary." I really had a great day, but I am doing terribly in maintaining this "healthy lifestyle" I have worked hard for over the past five months. Now, I'm spending more days eating poorly than eating well. It's going to catch up with me if I don't stop.

5.11.2019

I felt lonely today. Irshaad went out and ran errands and went to the movies with his mother. I was home with the children, and I grew weary of them. Days like today, I feel like a bad mom, a mean mom, a selfish mom. These children did not ask to be here, and I worry that every dismissal and "no" hurts them. I'm reading a story about abuse. I am a product of abuse. I don't want them to resent me.

5.12.2019

Today is Mother's Day, and I had probably one of the best Mother's Days I can recall. My husband bought me an aloe plant, and it was a perfect gift. I have been wanting to have house plants for a while but have put off buying something like that for myself. I'm so proud of my hubby. Miyah made me some incredible things for Mother's Day that I will treasure always. I spoke with my mama; she's doing OK. I sent some Mother's Day cards to my mommy friends, mom, and sister, and I also did a mommy mail swap with women from a writing platform I'm on. I really enjoy sending out letters. This snail mail thing is a lost art. Anyway, I had a great day, and I was relaxed. The house was finally clean, and I felt loved, wanted, and appreciated. That's what it's all about.

5.13.2019

Irshaad is in pain; his mouth is throbbing. I made him an appointment to go to the dentist tomorrow. I hate seeing him in pain. I've never been in pain like that with my teeth before. Miyah's belly is bothering her again. I rescheduled her follow up with the gastro because I was supposed to take her to get an X-ray and have her poop tested, and I did neither. I'm also scared shitless of driving back to that doctor's office. I went to Walmart today and brought Angel with me. I had a panic attack on my way there. Stopping at red lights on that busy-ass congested road makes me so anxious. It's been a while since I had one, and it's been a long time since I had one that fucking bad. I can't wait to get back on my meds.

5.14.2019

Meh

5.15.2019

I sent out my request for my transcripts today, but now, I'm not sure what field I want to concentrate on. Both options are in the same field but are on totally different school paths. The drug and alcohol counselor path doesn't follow the typical class credits; it's solely focused on addiction counseling and education. I still have time to decide, but I need to decide soon. Irshaad got to see the dentist today. He is having a tooth pulled on Monday. My own tooth that got filled is feeling weird as hell. There is a hole in my tooth that wasn't there before, and food gets stuck in it a lot. The exposed part of the hole is sensitive to cold and hot food, probably since it's been sheltered by my other teeth its entire life. What did this dentist do to me?

5.16.2019

Spent close to three hours detangling, washing, deep-conditioning, re-detangling, and styling Miyah's hair today. I should have done all this last weekend, but I was too lazy. I had to get it done because she has a birthday party to go to on Saturday. Angel's hair also needs TLC, as well as my locs. Black hair care is something else.

5.17.2019

Miyah and Angel finally got to see the dentist today. Both have been complaining of tooth pain, but we were told that neither have cavities. Honestly, I was expecting them to have a couple between the two of them. The girls had a good experience getting their teeth cleaned, so I'm happy about that. When we were out, we ran into one of Irshaad's union bosses, and he said he called Irshaad about a local job yesterday. We came home and saw that he called the house phone. I was in the house with the baby when his boss called, but I had no idea. He was pretty pissed at me for a couple of minutes for missing out on a job, but he let it go. I'm glad because it was an honest mistake. Luckily, he was understanding. I do wonder how long it will be until he is called into another job.

5.18.2019

Miyah went to her first birthday party for a classmate this year. I RSVP'd, and Miyah has been looking forward to it ever since. She had such a great time, and I was happy to be there for her. I was a mess, dreading this event the past few days. It sounds insane (because it is), but I was so worried about being around a bunch of strangers and just being uncomfortable and socially awkward. I was even thinking about my career choice, like *Dana, why do you want to be in human services when you're afraid of being around humans?* BB made me feel better about it. She's expecting baby number three, by the way. I'm so happy for my best friend! She's hoping for a girl, and so am I. I was just looking at pictures from around this time last year when I was pregnant. I was round and miserable. I also had terrible insomnia. Almost every night, I was waking up to numbing sensations in my leg and arm. I'm glad all that stuff is behind me.

5.19.2019

I haven't been taking the time to write at all. I haven't read this past week, either. I read a great book and feel like I can't really let it go and move on until I write a review on Instagram. I am having trouble writing a review, though. I stepped on the scale, and I am back in the 130s. I can't even tell you the last time I was there. Maybe when Miyah was a baby? I feel great; I love the way I look. My tummy is still here, but it's shrinking at its own rate, I guess. At this point, I've lost almost thirty pounds. I have my workout class tomorrow with BB. I haven't been in, like, four weeks, and I haven't been eating right lately, either. I'm so worried about trying to maintain how far I've come. I also have to do laundry, and I have my writer's meeting tonight. Happy Sunday.

5.20.2019

There is a volunteer opportunity coming up, and I have been considering going for it. Then, I found out volunteering requires twenty hours of training. I can't swing that right now. I haven't spent that much time away from my baby, and I'm still not ready to yet. I feel like the timing just isn't right, but will it ever be? Is there another organization I can try and get into? I really like the idea of this one and what they do for women and families, but if the timing isn't right, what can I do? Or am I just making excuses again?

5.21.2019

I found myself back at the dentist yet again to get a filling done and to fix the one that fell out. I had another panic attack after the numbing medicine took effect, and the dentist left, saying she would be back in a few minutes. After waiting for about five minutes to see if I was going into cardiac arrest and nothing happened, I was able to chill out. Then, the dentist declared that my remaining cavities are just in the enamel and they won't be filling them unless they get worse. I didn't speak up and say, "Lady, my teeth hurt!" I just ate a brownie, and it still causes pain in, like, two teeth. So, obviously, I have to go back.

5.22.2019

Irshaad's and my eyes were opened up when we started working the numbers for daycare. The rates are outrageous, and we would have to double it for both of the younger children. I have a friend who runs a daycare right outside her home, but it's in the opposite direction of my school. Her rates are workable, though. BB watching the girls is an option, but she's pregnant, and I worry that she might not be up for it, even if she says she is at first.

5.23.2019

I went to the park with the girls today. It was Aaliyah's very first time, and she smiled so big and wide when I put her in the baby swing. I finally broke through a wall that was keeping me from finishing a writing piece. I dropped the essay for weeks and stopped writing altogether. I'm back now and hope to have this finished to submit to my writer's group.

5.24.2019

We got back from taking the girls to NYC for the Trolls Experience. They had such a great time, and I had the worst panic attack of my life, times two. Going to and leaving the city was absolute hell for me. I was completely out of control. The fear had such a grip over me, and I tried to have fun in the city. It felt good walking on the streets and enjoying the sun and culture, but I kept thinking about the drive home. I kept thinking about how terrible the ride there was. Why was it so bad? I get myself so worked up that I can't come down. The only thing that can stop the attack is getting out of the vehicle, but I feel trapped. My body keeps telling me something is going to happen to me, despite so much evidence telling me otherwise. And now that I'm home, I'm so filled with shame, so sorry I had to add that stress on to my husband. It's bad enough that I don't do long-distance driving so he has to do it every time we venture out, but for me to be freaking out in the passenger seat, squeezing his hands for two hours, is too much.

I kept wishing I never agreed to go on the trip. I kept thinking I will never leave my town again and will feel perfectly fine doing just that. I kept wishing I could just stay in the city so I didn't have to go back on the highway and the bridge. But my kids had a good time, and they don't know Mommy freaked out. I'm terrified they will see my panic attacks in action one day, and God forbid I pass this neurosis on to them.

5.25.2019

I'm still reeling from yesterday. I even struggled to go to sleep last night. I want to talk to my mom about it. I want to see my therapist sooner than our appointment is scheduled for. I need to see the psychiatrist sooner, too. I need to get this shit under control. We are supposed to go on a trip to Hershey, Pennsylvania in July. I can't freak out for a four-hour car ride. I might kill myself from the stress. I'm scared.

5.26.2019

I have come to the realization that I really need to work on my people skills, especially if I dare to find work in the human services field. I have been in a few situations lately, like mom events, park trips, Angel's storytime, Miyah's field day, where I had the chance to connect with other moms and people, and I chose not to. I don't like to talk to people I don't know, and it doesn't feel natural. But I can no longer use that as an excuse to be quiet. I'm not saying I'm going to change overnight, but I need to practice. I've been home with my children for almost four years. My people skills need work, just like my muscles.

5.27.2019

We just came from BB's house, and I had such a fun, relaxing time with my best friend and our families. I had my favorite food, cheeseburgers from the grill, and my first adult beverage in two years. It was nice. When we were alone, I told her about my panic attack, and she was supportive as always, which I appreciated. She also confessed to me that she struggles with getting behind the wheel as well. She was in an accident last summer, and it's been fucking with her ever since. I'm glad she told me this and also explained why she hasn't been around to see Aaliyah and me as often as she said she would, which has honestly bothered me. I'm glad I have a best friend that understands me when few people actually do.

5.28.2019

Mom is one month sober. Congratulations, Mama! I have to bring Miyah back to the gastro in two days, and I am dreading it. On our way to BB's yesterday, I started to panic at the last light before her house. Thankfully, Irshaad didn't realize it, or he didn't say anything if he did. I'm anticipating this drive being terrible, and I'm already setting myself up for failure. I wish so bad that I didn't have these fears, that I could go places just like everyone else. Truth is I rescheduled this appointment twice already because I was afraid, and I can't do that anymore. My anxiety is really beginning to take over my life, and I can't let it. I shared my woes on social media and was given some support from friends and strangers. A lot of people told me to be strong and stay strong. I don't feel strong. Not at all.

5.29.2019

Bumped heads with my stepson today, as we do every so often. Sometimes I go soft on him and feel like he's not getting enough structure or discipline. Sometimes I put my foot down and worry that he might hate me. I always wonder if I'm doing the right thing. I love him and want the best for him, no matter what. I'm shitting a brick for Miyah's gastro appointment tomorrow.

5.30.2019

Took Miyah to see her gastro across the "scary" bridge and the merge that scares the crap out of me. We got there without incident. I was very anxious but was able to calm myself. The appointment went well; I will be taking her back at the end of the month (yay). We got lost taking the stairs instead of the elevator on the way out. Typical Dana. The whole clan then went to see *Aladdin* at the movies and got Taco Bell. I was able to eat Taco Bell while sitting in my car with my door open and occasionally stepping out. Will I ever eat like a normal fucking person again?

5.31.2019

Irshaad was sent back out to work for an undetermined amount of time. I was in a really shit mood all day. The day is almost done, and a dark cloud is still over me. I spoke to my dad today. He got on my nerves, but I still ordered him a Father's Day gift online. I tried to get in to see my psychiatrist earlier, but nothing was available. I'm stressed about this four-hour car ride. I'm doing this to myself. Working myself up like I did yesterday. Will this shit never end?

june

2019

Currently

LOVING new opportunities

MAKING the dots connect

READING ¯meh¯

THINKING and not speaking

EATING yummy things

WISHING for happiness

HATING haters that hate

PLANNING so many projects

DRINKING water and coffee. my drug of choice

WANTING to be free

6.1.2019

June, what's good?

6.2.2019

Broke Miyah's heart today when I finally told her I can't chaperone her trip. She bawled, and I felt terrible. If I'm being entirely transparent, I'm relieved I don't have to watch a bunch of kids that probably won't listen to me and interact with adults I don't like. Was that as pathetic as it sounded? I thought so.

6.3.2019

Am I an introvert because I'm a writer, or am I a writer because I'm an introvert? No matter how bad things get sometimes, I feel so hopeful when I press the pen to paper. That's freedom.

I recently discovered I have intrusive thoughts. It's not that they just started happening; I now have a definition for what they are. I will not be sharing them out loud. Or even on paper. Think of the terrible things.

6.4.2019

New gig. Funnily enough, it involves driving.

6.5.2019

Baby Aaliyah will be nine months old tomorrow.

6.6.2019

Miyah was in more pain than I have ever seen last night. It was terrible. I finally got her to sleep by rubbing her back, but her pain continued when she woke up. I took her to the ER, and she started feeling better, so we were discharged. I was made to feel like I shouldn't have brought her there at all since she has a gastro already, and we have some sort of plan in place. I honestly didn't know what else to do, though. She didn't even go to school today. We went to the park for an hour soon after, and I've been trying my best to keep her happy and busy. I'm terrified that tonight is going to play out the same way.

6.7.2019

I am at the library with my girls today. We walked because it is a stunning day outside. Miyah was in pain again last night, and she was writhing in pain, so we went back to the ER (twice in one day for those counting). They checked her pee, did an X-ray, and sent us home. Irshaad and I decided to put her on a gluten-free diet while we await the endoscopy her gastro suggested. Miyah had pains this morning as well but is now feeling fine. I'm anxiously anticipating her pain being back tonight for the third night in a row. Please stop this pain, dear God. It hurts not being able to help her at all. I am thinking the cause might be IBS, but I'm not sure, nor is her doctor.

6.8.2019

I drove to Dennis's dad's funeral by myself today. I don't think I could have done it without navigation on my phone, but it felt good to be independent and not have to force Irshaad to bring the kids and come with me because I'm too afraid to drive. I need to get this practice because I will be driving to quite a few unfamiliar places because of my new gig. What I'm doing is basically driving to certain retailers and posting paid advertisements on these little sanitizer booths. It's a super easy job, and the pay is twenty bucks a store. I went to a few stores this weekend, and I know exactly where a couple more are. Irshaad took the girls with him to play ball, and Miyah came home happy. I'm hopeful that switching her to a gluten-free diet is helping. I guess we shall see tonight.

6.9.2019

It's Monday morning, and I woke up with a pit in my stomach. Miyah was in pain again last night for hours. I tried to distract her and keep her happy and positive, but this is fucking hard. I have a few phone calls to make today for her. I'm dreading that she is going to wake up happy, only to come to me minutes later saying, "Mommy, my belly hurts." I was so stressed all weekend. My first actual meal wasn't until spaghetti last night. I don't know what to do.

6.10.2019

Random Gratitude Thread:

- loving husband
- wonderful children
- a roof over my head
- indoor plumbing
- new job opportunity
- my writing group

6.11.2019

I took Angel and Aaliyah to the park for story time. Believe it or not, we still have the stroller from when *Miyah* was a baby. It still works, but it is torn up! It's embarrassing to be around all the soccer moms with their three-wheeled strollers and take-out coffees. My daughters and I are the only people of color, and we stick out like a sore thumb—not that I'm not used to it.

6.12.2019

Eh, another day.

6.13.2019

Prepping Miyah's hair for her performance tomorrow. I can't believe my baby is almost done with kindergarten.

6.14.2019

Miyah's Kindergarten "Extravaganza" was today. I love my baby. She looked beautiful, and I enjoyed seeing her, but this district needs to work on their productions! Us parents were packed into the auditorium; there weren't even enough chairs for everyone. Each class had their kids line up, repeat some passages, then sing a song. And by "sing a song," I mean scream at the top of their lungs with no music accompanying them as they shrieked in an unintelligible manner. After that, it was abruptly over. We took pictures and left. I was just seriously underwhelmed. I went to a magnet elementary school that used to blow the house down during performances, so maybe I'm biased.

6.15.2019

I was looking at pictures from this time last year. My mama was here visiting, and I had a big ole pregnant belly. I was completely miserable throughout my pregnancy, and I was convinced it would kill me. But here I am, a mother of three wonderful girls and a stepmama to an awesome son. I'm still here. I hope life gets better.

6.16.2019

Happy Father's Day, Irshaad, a man who was never afraid to change diapers, who always does his part, and has a great relationship with all his children, which is so important. I love you.

6.17.2019

Why do we have no sense of humanity or even a little empathy for people who are different from us?

6.18.2019

The month is more than halfway over, and it is time for me to start venturing off to the places I'm less familiar with for my driving gig. I'm nervous, and it is raining today. The place is literally all the way up the street from my house and close to my new school, so this is going to be a good experience for me. But I'm scared. I egged myself on and deliberately asked for these cities for a reason. Time to stop being scared of the unknown—in life and on the roads.

6.19.2019

So, today was fucking rough. I woke up happy and chillin', took Q to the high school for his eighth grade graduation practice, got Miyah up and off to school, and cleaned the girls' room. I called to confirm my appointment with the psychiatrist and realized, to my sheer horror, that the appointment was yesterday. I spent the next two hours in tears, trying to amend my mistake and maybe get seen somewhere else. I've come to the realization that no one cares. I made the appointment over a month in advance and have been struggling with my anxiety and eating so much lately, but none of that matters. As of right now, I'm on "standby," which doesn't really mean shit, and I have a new appointment for the fifteenth of July, just after my vacation. I'm hopeful I can be seen before then and start my meds before my vacation. I'm hopeful it's going to all work out, but I don't know.

6.20.2019

So many things are causing me stress at the moment. Our vacation is two weeks from Saturday, and I'm terrified of the car ride there, but I'm trying to come up with a plan and also mentally prepare myself. I have four more stores to check on before the month ends, and three out of the four are in a spot I am completely unfamiliar with. I'm pretty scared, like I was the other day.

I got my stores done but was panicked almost the entire time, thinking I was going to be lost and stranded where I was. I was gone for about two hours and spent most of that time silently freaking out. I had to push myself to get it done, but I did get it done. I also have to get my FAFSA done, as well as my placement tests for school. I have mother mail to send out, a few cards to send, and stuff for Miyah's teachers, bus driver, etc. to get ready. I'm shitting a brick. No word about a new appointment, either. I'm still in disbelief that I let this happen.

6.21.2019

Miyah's first year of school is ending in just a few days. I am looking forward to having fun this summer. Our vacation is very close, and everyone is excited. I still don't know how I'm going to do this without medicine. A four-hour panic attack might just kill me.

6.22.2019

I wish I had time to gather my thoughts
at home,
alone.
Lay in bed.
Stare at the ceiling.
Cry.
Have time to examine the pain I'm feeling.
Scream and let go.
Blast music I know.
Take a shower in peace,
thirty minutes at least.
Air-dry
at my own leisure,
not the typical get-back-to-housework procedure (never finished).

6.23.2019

BB and I had a bit of a falling out because of some very personal stuff. I wish the whole situation never happened. I'm a little hurt, but I know she is, too. And, really, the situation didn't even involve us.

Well, today is probably the worst day of my life. I say that with certainty and shame. I caused an accident today that could have killed me. I reacted like an ass and waited until I drove home to call the cops. It happened on a bridge, and the other vehicle was a semi-truck. God literally saved my life today because I could have not made it home to my family. Instead, I didn't even get a scratch. Wow, if I thought I knew what shame was before today, I did not. I did this, forcing myself to get into the car and onto the damn bridge, to do my side hustle gig, and I was scared, but I kept telling myself I could do it. Look what happened.

The day is nearly over, and I still can't believe how all the events played out. I hate myself today.

I can't wait until all of this is just a distant memory. But there are a few things that need to be taken care of immediately, and I don't know how I'm going to get through everything with this hanging onto me. The evidence is on my car and is a symbol of my life, fucked. I will be explaining what happened to countless friends and families in the next few months. This is so embarrassing. I need to be grateful I am fucking alive. I could be fucking dead right now, and it would have been one hundred percent my fault. Why am I so careless all the time? I think it was a teachable moment. I have to always be careful. Always. I don't want to give up the gig that caused this accident, either. This situation is designed to break me, to make my anxiety worse, to make me lose all confidence. I know the only way to beat it is to keep pushing. But I also know myself. Can I do this? Yes. Will I?

6.26.2019

Woke up feeling pretty OK. Now, my stomach is in knots. I'm terrified of nothing and everything. I don't want to lose this gig, but the thought of going anywhere when I am not sure where I am going is so stressful; I can barely calm myself down. I keep telling myself it is all in my head and I will be fine, but I don't really believe myself. I keep trying to prove to myself that this is a mind-over-matter thing. But is it really?

6.27.2019

It's Irshaad's birthday. We're going to our favorite food spot across the bridge. Not the one I almost died on, but still, I'm scared. Sorry I can't be a normal person on your birthday, baby.

I just realized that when I got into my accident the other day, my father was the first person I called.

6.28.2019

So, I am here at the library, trying to calm myself down. I've been an emotional wreck all day. I'm terrified of working myself up so much that I might give myself a fucking stroke.

Dana Muwwakkil

This has been the worst week of my life. The worst part is, right now, I am freaking out about things that haven't even happened yet. I'm so stressed about doing my remaining stores (even with Irshaad driving me). I desperately sent my boss an email asking her if I can push those stores to next month. Luckily, she agreed and was very supportive. I laid all my cards on the table, which I will admit is not professional, but I don't know what else to do. I cried to both my mother and brother today. They both suffer from anxiety, and they were both supportive. My brother is going to be sending me some all-natural stuff he takes sometimes, and I am desperate enough to try that as well. At this point, I just need to do whatever I can to get through the car ride for my vacation.

This shit is so bad; I can now relate when people say "I wouldn't wish this on my worst enemy." My anxiety keeps spiraling, and I feel like I'm losing it.

6.29.2019

I didn't feel like getting out and being social today, but I'm glad we went to celebrate our friend's daughter's birthday. I experienced a bit of social awkwardness and uneasiness, but the sentiments were normal compared to how this week has been fucking with me.

I got to sit with Fatima and have girl talk for a little while, and that was great for my spirit as well.

I went to yoga today, and there was a different instructor. I felt a bit out of my element and found it hard to concentrate. On the way home, I wanted to stay on the highway and cross the bridge where I had my accident, but I didn't have the balls to face my fear. I then came home and spiraled some more. I could not calm down until I worked out and had my writer's meeting. It was a great meeting, and I felt so much lighter after. Now, it's the evening, and I'm exhausted. Six days until vacation, and I should be stressed but excited. I just keep thinking about losing it for four hours in the car on the way there.

A quote from our yoga instructor today:
"Each morning, we are born again…" —Buddha

july

2019

Currently

LOVING the man I married

MAKING things right: I have to

READING can't

THINKING about What if?

EATING What's that?

WISHING

HATING myself

PLANNING

DRINKING *sigh* Yes. I am

WANTING

7.1.2019

It's July.

7.2.2019

Finally got to see my therapist, and I completely lost it while I was in her office. I couldn't stop crying. I told her all my fears, and she listened, but I left disappointed. I think I was hoping she would save me somehow. I was hoping she would provide me with the ultimate solution for getting through this drive, but she didn't. She did give me more tools, some grounding techniques, and more paperwork, but I can't imagine any of it actually working. How am I going to get through this?

7.3.2019

Today, I woke up and felt OK for a little while until the familiar sense of dread crept in. I have been doing a lot of cleaning because nothing else keeps me distracted enough. At this rate, I am obsessed with my anxiety. The trip is still days away, and I am wishing we never booked it. What the hell was I thinking? This is exactly why I didn't want to go to Disney World.

7.4.2019

I feel a little bit better today. I spent most of my time bingeing season three of *Stranger Things* with Irshaad, and we took the girls outside for sparklers and poppers. I drank a bit today, and it helped ease my mind. I am feeling a lot more at peace with the situation. I am trying to be excited. Happy Fourth?

7.5.2019

D-Day is tomorrow. Doing last-minute packing and trying not to panic. I have a survival bag with books, journals, and all the paperwork my therapist has given me. I have nail polish and a manicure kit. I have all the stuff so I can retwist my locs on the way there, and we have a playlist of all my favorite music ready to go. The kids are excited. Irshaad is so hyped. I wish I was, too.

7.6.2019

Hello, Hershey, PA. I cannot believe I made it without an anxiety attack. I did not look at the road for the most part. I sang the entire time and kept my hands busy while doing my hair and nails. Somehow, I made it. I almost gave in to negative thoughts when we took our break and Irshaad started freaking out because our car was making strange noises. Luckily, there wasn't an actual problem, but him becoming unhinged almost took me there. I wanted to yell at him, but he has the right to get worried and freak out, too. I'm feeding Aaliyah, then the kids and I are heading to the hotel pool and jacuzzi.

7.7.2019

I woke up today to my right ear thudding in pain. There were a lot of rambunctious assholes in the pool last night, and although I didn't submerge my head underwater at all, I was splashed so much that some water has become trapped in my ear. I feel like an asshole because I was made to feel uncomfortable, and instead of saying something, I just left. I also feel incredibly anxious. I am forcing myself to eat so I can have some fuel, but my fear of choking has soared in this new place. We went out for pizza last night, and I could only manage a few bites before I quit. We aren't going to the park until the evening, but we are going to be tourists and walk around, and I'm sure we will end up at the pool. I'm already thinking about the drive home, and it's taking me out of the moment. I hate this.

I was a big ball of worry today because I am now continuing to obsess about our drive home. We drove up a very windy mountain that made my ears pop, and I'm shocked it didn't freak me out. I am fearful it's going to kill me on the way home. We are going to Hershey Park tonight, and I am dreading that as well. I just want to go home. I hate this trip, and I can't burden Irshaad by telling him my true feelings. I keep pretending I'm OK, but I'm internally screaming.

7.8.2019

We went to the park last night, and I had a great time. I was finally able to take my mind off my negative thoughts, and seeing my children laughing and smiling made me genuinely feel good for the first time in a while. We were having so much fun until it started pouring. Then, we had to make a mad dash to our car with hundreds of other people, something that might be anxiety-inducing, but I was OK. What a night it was. I am waiting to get into the shower to calm my nerves before we go back to the park today. We are wearing matching shirts I got from Etsy. I love my family.

7.9.2019

Today was our last day at the park, and we had fun. Yesterday was probably the best day, and we really maximized our time. Today was more laidback, and we hung out at the water park. I'm completely exhausted, almost too tired to worry about getting on the road tomorrow. Almost.

7.10.2019

We are back in New York. I am happy to report that I made it anxiety free. I am so relieved to be back in my home; also thrilled that we left it in decent condition. I'm anxious to get back into my workout routine, take my girls to do fun things, and enjoy our summer. The sad thing is, because of my accident, our trip gave me so much worry that I put things I enjoy on hold. And although I didn't have anxiety on the road, I spent the days leading up to the trip and the days during the trip in constant worry. I was so stressed, my legs ached. There were moments when the fear was so great that my arm went numb. My anxiety kept me from truly enjoying myself. And I hate myself for letting this happen.

7.11.2019

I reached out to a friend today to ask for advice on the aloe Irshaad bought me on Mother's Day, my first plant. She's grown a lot since I was gifted her, but something is wrong. She's drying out or something. I am going to keep her outside for now.

7.12.2019

I started to share this diary/project with my writing group. They were pretty riveted by it, I think. I'm still thinking about a title. I am thinking about calling it *Three Six Five* (or *365*). It would make sense, but it certainly isn't eye-catching or interesting.

7.13.2019

I feel anxious again for no reason. Why?

7.14.2019

I left my aloe on the porch in the rain today. When I remembered to get her, she was completely drowned and limp.

7.15.2019

I went to see my new psychiatrist today. BB watched the girls for me, and on my way out the door, she said, "Enjoy yourself." Unfortunately, it was not that type of appointment.

It was finally my evaluation. First, a medical assistant took my blood pressure, and she announced it was *really* high. It scared the crap out of me. I could barely focus on my appointment, especially because when my psychiatrist looked at my stats, she couldn't believe my blood pressure was so high; she assured me it was wrong. I spent our time crying while talking about my history with anxiety and medication and all of my triggers. I was a wreck. My blood pressure was taken again, and it was still high. I was given a new prescription. It's different from the meds I was on last year, but I will give it a try. I can't wait for some relief.

7.16.2019

I started my new meds this morning. I now have a new obsession: worrying about my blood pressure. I feel weird so far, and I'm afraid I will have a stroke. I talked to mom, and she made me feel better about my blood pressure. She actually has hypertension and has had it since age forty.

7.17.2019

Another day of obsessing. I'm seeing a doctor tomorrow about my ear, which has been hurting since our trip, and I plan on bringing up my blood pressure. I've been trying to be normal today. I need to get back to things I used to do. I took the girls to the library. We were there for an hour, and even the baby had a good time exploring the children's area. I'm going to review a story from my writer's group, prep dinner, and work out.

7.18.2019

I had a physical today, and my blood pressure went down. It's still a little high but not nearly as high as it was, so I feel such relief. I'm still waiting to get back to my lovely summer, have fun, do things with my girls, and work out. Hopefully, I can get back on track.

7.19.2019

Something is wrong with my brain. My legs have been bothering me today, and they were all I could think about. I keep thinking I have a blood clot.

7.20.2019

Today, I am obsessing about a slight pressure I'm feeling on the right side of my head. I hate this medicine, and I hate my body for trying to adjust to it. I hate this so much. I hate everything. Lately, I am having very low points in my day where I just feel hopeless. I feel worthless. I feel useless, like I will never be better, and soon, everyone will know how shitty I am. Then, it passes. I hope these types of thoughts are not here to stay.

7.21.2019

I went wine tasting with Fatima today. I was incredibly anxious in the morning, but once I started getting ready and playing music, I felt like myself, my happy self. We were out for hours, and I had a great time getting to know my friend even better. We went to get Chinese food after the tasting. I ate two pieces of sweet and sour chicken. Fatima complimented me on how skinny I look. I wanted to tell her it's the stress diet.

7.22.2019

I spent hours outside with the girls today and let them play with the water table. I've been feeling this weird anxiousness in the late morning/early afternoon. I think it's the medicine. It doesn't last all day, but it's such a weird feeling, like I can't relax, and my mind is racing. I hope it stops soon.

7.23.2019

Why did I let this lady give me this medicine? Will my body adjust or not? I feel better when I go outside for walks or just sit on the porch in the sun. I have my placement test for school tomorrow. I kept putting it off, but I can't any longer. I need to get it over with so I can pick my classes. I will be starting college in a few weeks. Maybe life can return to normal.

7.24.2019

I got up at 7:30 feeling nervous about my test. I made myself coffee and crammed in some last-minute studying as the girls woke up. Irshaad got up so he could fix everyone breakfast, and we were on our way. He drove me because the campus is about forty minutes away, and I'm not comfortable doing it alone yet. About ten minutes into our drive, I completely lost it with my anxiety. I started crying and begged Irshaad to take me back home. He tried to stay neutral and asked if I was sure, but I know he was disappointed. I rescheduled the test before we even got back home. I need to redeem myself. Once again, I must ask myself: *Is it the medicine?*

7.25.2019

I'm not giving my body enough nutrients or calories, and my weight is continuing to drop. I'm still feeling anxious every day. My plan is to walk to the post office to send out some friend mail, then go to the library for about an hour. I'm contemplating if I should bring the girls. I know they would enjoy the walk and the library. I need to be selfish and give myself some solitude.

I'm at the library now, but I did not walk. I got into a huge argument with Irshaad. He was so mad, he was shaking. I know I am taking a toll on him. I am so sorry.

7.26.2019

Irshaad and I are not in a good place right now. I'm not just carrying this anxiety for myself; I'm carrying it for him. I have literally *ruined* events for us and made them unenjoyable because of my anxiety. Our third wedding anniversary was on a cruise in NYC, and I had an anxiety attack the entire time. I still haven't forgiven myself for that. He puts up with a lot from me, and I do not blame him for being on edge because of my anxiety.

7.27.2019

Irshaad took me to take my placement test. The ride is very simple. The campus is simple and kind of ugly. The closer we got, the more I started to freak out in the car. I had to gather myself for a few minutes before I went inside. I know I did well on the essay portion, and I did well with the reading as well, but I choked on the math. I did better than I thought I would do, but I was still placed in a non-credit math class. I had to fight off an anxiety attack on the way home. I have to do laundry tonight. I made plans with a friend to meet for coffee and go to Barnes & Noble today, but I'm going to flake.

7.28.2019

Met Fatima at yoga, which was intense but very relaxing. Then, I picked up groceries and came home to fold laundry. I've been terribly anxious ever since I felt a cooling sensation on the side of my head for a few moments. I'm very irritable but trying not to snap at the kids or Irshaad. To try and keep busy, I've washed the dishes, swept, and watched a few vlogs. I'm getting ready to take the girls outside to play in the water table. I think the fresh air and watching the three of them have fun will help me. I'm moderating my writer's meeting tonight. I'm excited and a little nervous.

Dana Muwwakkil

7.29.2019

My day started off pretty rocky. I woke up with a pit in my stomach again and started manually breathing. It drove me crazy for hours. By two p.m., I was tired, irritable, and feeling sorry for myself, and I have to stop doing that. Things could be so much worse. I took the girls to play outside, which helped chill me out, then I put the baby down for a nap. I then put the older two in their room for quiet time, which gave me a little over an hour to decompress. And I felt a lot better after that. I needed that mental break because Irshaad is back at work, and I'm home alone. I feel somewhat like myself. I started my cleaning routine again and spent most of the day deep cleaning.

7.30.2019

"We're all mad here."

7.31.2019

Dear, God, let August be better.

august

August 2019

Currently

- LOVING

- MAKING

- READING

- THINKING

- EATING

- WISHING

- HATING

- PLANNING

- DRINKING

- WANTING

8.1.2019

God, grant me the serenity
to accept the things I cannot change,
the courage to change the things I can,
and the wisdom to know the difference.

8.2.2019

Journal Prompt: List your favorite words.

Cafe
Black
Expeditiously
Genuine
Love
Revolutionary
Empathy

8.3.2019

I thought I hit bottom before, but I think today was the day. I kept plans with one of my writer friends to meet for coffee and talk about writing and books at Barnes & Noble. I was already feeling anxious before I left. I had major anxiety at the stoplight right around the corner. I didn't even feel fully present during our conversation because I started to feel anxious again. I left abruptly, saying I had to do something for my kids or something. I did not browse books or even get my favorite cafe mocha. I panicked on the way home, too, and told Irshaad what happened when I got home.

He confessed to me that my mental state is putting so much stress on him, and that he's frankly terrified. He thinks I should go into a facility. "You need time to be alone and figure stuff out for you as Dana. Not as a mother or wife but as a person. You are losing yourself." I won't say that, during the past few months, the thought never entered my mind because it has. It would be easier to digest all of this and work on myself alone. But I don't feel like it's an option. I wish I could have someone at home who could help us so I can recover. Hearing my husband say those words out loud literally brought me off the couch to lie on the floor. I just feel defeated.

"I can't believe this is my life," I said.

My husband joined me on the floor and held my hand. "We will get through this," he told me.

Please, God, make it true.

8.4.2019

Journal Prompt: What simple pleasures do you enjoy most?

A delicious cup of coffee with a book and/or a blank piece of paper and a pen.

8.5.2019

Journal Prompt: Describe yourself in ten words.

1. Simple
2. Empathetic
3. Proud
4. Pro-Black
5. Unsure
6. Mama
7. Nerd
8. Evolving
9. Scribe
10. Thoughtful

8.6.2019

Journal Prompt: Do you tell the truth, even if it might hurt?
No. I wish I did.

8.7.2019

Miyah is supposed to have a breath test tomorrow in Westchester. I can't take her. I don't think she's lactose intolerant anyway.

8.8.2019

I just want to be normal again. What about the Dana I was ten years ago? What happened to me? Even the Dana I was five years ago. She's gone.

8.9.2019

BB

You seemed really quiet today. Are you OK?

Dana

Not really

BB

Is it your medicine? You were not like this before.

Dana

I don't know.

8.10.2019

I'm writing this because I promised I would write every day.

8.11.2019

I see my doc again tomorrow.

8.12.2019

I just got home. I am going off this medicine while going back onto the one that worked for me before. I should have put my foot down last month and made her put me on this one then. I wasted a month and suffered because I thought she knew what was best for me. I start the new meds tomorrow night.

8.13.2019

I just took my new meds, and I'm going to sleep.

8.14.2019

So far, so good, but I'm on high alert for side effects.
A new school year is upon us. I am almost done school
shopping for Miyah and Q. Mimi is going to the first grade,
and Q is going to be a freshman!

8.15.2019

I woke up last night in a bit of a panic. It was quite scary. I
was able to get myself back to sleep, but maybe I should start
taking my pill in the morning instead.

8.16.2019

It happened again last night. I was able to calm down, but it
took me over an hour to get back to sleep. I called my doctor,
and she said it's perfectly fine to take my meds in the morning
as long as I'm consistent.

8.17.2019

I've been getting that anxious feeling in my stomach again.
After going through a month of side effects with my old
meds, I'm almost used to this feeling by now. But when will
it go away? When will I be able to wake up and just be?

8.18.2019

I finally feel like my appetite is back. I'm actually hungry. I
want to eat, and I have been eating without fear for the first
time in a long time. Headache all day.

8.19.2019

For the first time in a great while, I ate until I was full.

8.20.2019

Headache all day.

8.21.2019

Manifest

Law of Attraction says you are what you attract,
so I'm tryna shake these demons,
but they keep pulling on my back.
Yes, I've been doing yoga;
Warrior 2, yeah, that's the one,
but I still can't find my center.
How much more unhinged will I become?

8.22.2019

I wish this fear would end. I wish this would subside. Why can't I be who I used to be? What happened to me?

8.23.2019

Trying to keep myself busy while getting school supplies and clothes ready for September. Cleaning the girls' room today.

8.24.2019

Things to look forward to when I get better:

- Going out with my husband
- Being able to travel without fear
- Having a good time with friends
- *Freedom*

8.25.2019

Miyah's gastro has come to the conclusion that she needs more fiber in her diet. After all we have been through—the stomach pains, the hospital visits, the bloodwork, and X-rays—all she needed was more fiber? Not to mention, she's been on a daily laxative most of the year.

8.26.2019

We met Miyah's friend and mother at a little farm near our house today. It was so nice to be out in the sunshine, talking to other people. Angel and Miyah played with Miyah's friend, and we all really enjoyed ourselves. Aaliyah was a good girl for me. She was also my safety net when I wanted to go home after about three hours. "She really needs her nap." I got a bit turned around on the way back, but I just pulled over and did my GPS like normal people do, even though I'm far from normal.

8.27.2019

Prepping for Angel's fourth birthday tomorrow!

8.28.2019

Angel is my feisty, fierce, sweet, and sensitive child. She is such a sweetheart and a brave little girl. I wanted her fourth birthday to be special. She woke up to balloons in her bed and all around the room. I bought her a pink dress; she *loves* dresses. I bought her unicorn sneakers and a matching headband. She got Barbies and some little stuff she will probably break within the week. We went to the park and the library today. We topped the night off with her favorite meal that I cook, chicken alfredo, and I made her an M&M's cake. Happy birthday to my Angel.

8.29.2019

Note to Self:

Hey, you're going to be OK. I don't know when, but you will be OK. Take these days one at a time. Read and write as much as you can. Eat and drink water and nourish your body. Go outside. Don't yell. I have faith in you. Irshaad, your mom, Drea, and BB have faith in you. Take care.

8.30.2019

I'm fine. Life is fine.

september

2019

Currently

LOVING the opportunity to renew

MAKING baby steps

READING no ... in a slump

THINKING dark thoughts

EATING with a healthy appetite

WISHING instead of doing

HATING uncertainty

PLANNING for a better year

DRINKING water

WANTING to be free

9.1.2019

OK, September. Let's do this.

9.2.2019

I had a really bad attack today. And the scariest part was I was at home doing nothing in particular. I was cleaning the girls' closet, then I just felt terror take over my body. I tried to ignore it. I tried to do deep breathing. I tried to distract myself. Irshaad wasn't at home, and I was home with the girls. I called my mom. When she called me back, she urged me to take my Ativan. I was so scared to take it.

"You have to try, Minnie," she said to me.

"I am trying, Mom," I said, with tears streaming down my face.

"That medicine is not going to hurt you. It will help you calm down."

I got off the phone with her and took my pill. I called her back, and we talked as I waited for it to kick in. I had calmed down by the time Irshaad came home twenty minutes later. That was such a terrifying experience because it wasn't one of my triggers that brought on the panic. I think it was my meds. Feeling anxious is something I have gotten used to, but a full-blown anxiety attack is not something I can do on a daily basis.

9.3.2019

I had a long talk with my psychiatrist over the phone. She told me not to beat myself up for taking a benzo because, apparently, I really needed it. I confessed about my fear of this happening every day. She suggested it might be lingering effects from my old medicine and this one. She couldn't guarantee that it wouldn't happen again. She also told me that some people use the benzos multiple times a day while they are adjusting to their antidepressants. It's just such a conundrum to me. She asked me if I wanted to stop altogether. I don't want to stop if I will be better soon.

9.4.2019

First day of first grade for Miyah and the first day of high school for Q! I'm so excited for them both. My Mimi is a first grader; I can't even believe it. I wish it was Angel's first year of school as well, but she has one more year home with Mommy. She always gets so sad when Miyah gets on the bus in the morning. She hangs her head and pouts all the way up the stairs. Your time will come soon, Angel. As for Q, I hope he really focuses this year. Each year, it's been the same; the teachers love him and say he has so much potential, but he seems uninterested in doing his work, although he is capable. Good luck, Mr. Freshman.

9.5.2019

And just like that, the first week of school is over. I had to run around like a mad woman this morning and take Q to get a physical so he can play in next week's game. It was stressful because I felt like if anything went wrong, it was going to be blamed on me. I encountered a nasty woman at the front desk, and I should have said something, but I didn't.

My dad met me at my house afterward. He got there before I could get back and clean up from the morning routine chaos before school. I tried to explain to him that my house doesn't always look like this, but he told me I didn't have to. We had a nice visit. I made burgers for lunch, and he fell asleep then went on his way. Love you, Dad.

9.6.2019

A year ago today, I gave birth to our last child, Aaliyah Renee Muwwakkil. When I found out I was pregnant, I spent a while in complete denial. And my pregnancy was hard. I was so tired; I spent the first three months in bed. Toward the end of my pregnancy, in the summer, I couldn't stand more than a few minutes without feeling like I was going to faint. I was miserable. I almost died after my C-section, and I lost so much blood due to complications; I had to have two transfusions. I was put to sleep, not knowing if I was going to wake up or become another black mother that died after giving birth. Obviously, I didn't die, but the ordeal brought all of my fears of mortality back to me. I believe it was the catalyst to my spiral. But despite all that, the rough pregnancy, labor, and recovery, it was all worth it because baby Aaliyah was meant to be here. I am blessed to have my third daughter. I am blessed because our family is complete.

9.7.2019

I spent the entire day in bed with stomach cramps, stomach bubbles, and nausea. I think the burgers I made myself and my dad a couple days ago were bad. I hope he's not sick, too, but I'm too embarrassed to call and ask him. Irshaad had to go help a friend move some stuff out of storage, and I was pissed he left me feeling shitty with the kids. He's back home now and rubbing me, so I feel better. I'm going to find something on YouTube and fall asleep.

9.8.2019

I have got to start writing again. I have been in a slump for damn near half of 2019 at this point, and it sucks. I had a goal to self-publish something this year, but I'm honestly not sure what I was thinking. Unless I plan on publishing a few rejected essays and poetry, I really have nothing.

9.9.2019

I finally took one of my vitamin D pills that was prescribed to me almost a month ago. I have been terrified that it will have an adverse effect on my anxiety medication. I woke up with a pit in my stomach again. I am slightly stressed out about a few normal errands that need to be done today. Irshaad isn't feeling too hot and is staying home today. That gives me some relief because I can leave the girls with him when I do my errands.

9.10.2019

Just got home from seeing my psychiatrist. She wants me to increase my dose, and I know it's necessary, but I'm fucking scared. After dealing with this since July, more weeks of anxiety that doesn't go away is very scary to me. I hate these side effects.

9.11.2019

I am so embarrassed. For about a week, I have been in correspondence with the website that is publishing my essay at the end of the month because I have incorrectly signed my contract several times. I just sent it again, and it's getting to a point where I'm suspecting they might call the whole thing off because I'm such a dumbass. I hope I do not have to hear from them again until it's time for my essay to go live.

9.12.2019

It's been a minute since I saw my best friend. We planned on watching a movie on Hulu but ended up shooting the shit, talking about her pregnancy and our kids for a few hours. It was such a nice time for me because I left the girls with Irshaad. I didn't realize how badly I needed time away from home.

9.13.2019

Just came home from a ladies' night event thingy at the movies with Fatima and Taibah. I had such a good time. I was gone for hours, having fun and chatting, until I realized I hadn't thought about my kids since I arrived. I also was anxiety free until the movie actually started. Then, I felt that anxious feeling in my stomach again. It went away soon after, but I felt it, almost like a reminder that my anxiety is always with me.

9.14.2019

I took my new pill (increased dose) over six hours ago, and so far, so good. In the back of my mind, I keep waiting for something bad to happen, for a wave of panic to come over me. I keep trying to challenge my thoughts. I opened up to Fatima about my anxiety last night for the first time, and I was surprised she could relate to me as well. It's so interesting finding out what others are actually going through when you share what you've been through.

9.15.2019

I'm outside with my daughters, enjoying these last few summer days. I woke up and went to yoga this morning, and the class was wonderful and challenging. Then, I picked up my groceries from Walmart and came home. Irshaad is usually running out the door to go ball when I get home on Sundays, but he stayed home today, and I'm happy. He's also laid off from work again.

I started feeling anxious a little while ago, not anxious enough to take an Ativan or anything; it's the familiar feeling I've gotten used to over these past eight weeks. I just hope my body adjusts to this dose quickly and this feeling doesn't get any more intense in the meantime.

9.16.2019

Kicking myself a little because I planned on spending a couple hours at the library, writing, making some cards to send out, and working on a flash fiction for my writer's group. I opted to stay home and basically do nothing all day. Irshaad is going back to work tomorrow, so I don't know when I will have another "free" day like the one I missed. My check came for my essay today, and instead of being excited, I almost didn't want to tell my husband about it. I want to go shopping really badly. I want to spend money on *me*, and I will spend most of my check on myself, but I guess I wish we were in a better space financially, where my writing check doesn't even need to be added to the pot. I know I'm being selfish, by the way.

9.17.2019

Guess where I am! Irshaad actually doesn't have work today; he goes in tomorrow. I couldn't let this opportunity pass me again, so I packed up my laptop, some paper and pens, and here I am at my local library. I am feeling anxious today. I am trying to ignore it. I found it a little hard to concentrate on my writing, but I can't let that stop me anymore. I haven't been on my groove since June. I need to get back to doing my thing. I need to start reading again. I've been looking back at my diary before I submit it to my writing group. Some of the things I have written are so embarrassing. The insecurity I internalize is not easy to admit to anyone, but I am sharing it anyway because I hope there are others out there who can relate to me. And maybe they will find comfort in knowing they are not alone.

9.18.2019

"Now is our time to change the world"—Common

9.19.2019

I felt pretty good today. Maybe I have adjusted.

9.20.2019

Never mind.

9.21.2019

I'm off to the library. It's been a while. I need to browse some books and sit in silence for a while. I wish I could just be home, alone and relaxing. I have to remember sometimes that this is motherhood, especially when you don't have family nearby. Do I sound selfish for wishing I had someone I could trust to watch our children for Irshaad and me? Wanting random weekends in bed because the kids are out with their aunts or grandparents? It's OK if I sound selfish. I feel how I feel.

9.22.2019

Sundays come and go too quickly. I really don't feel like writing.

9.23.2019

Still don't.

9.24.2019

I'm already thinking of things to get the girls for Christmas. Every year, I think I'm ahead of the game for the holidays, but I always end up stressed and annoyed. I do get the kids what they want, though.

9.25.2019

My very first published essay debuted online today! I am so incredibly proud of myself and, if I'm being honest, a little nervous about how it will be received. I am sharing something deeply personal with the world, and it's hard to share these intimate feelings with people who actually know me. The essay is pretty long, so that might actually deter a lot of people from reading it, but that's not really what I want. I want others who have gone through what I've gone through to know they are not alone. My mother has applauded me, so have many of my Facebook friends. As a writer, this gives me hope. I hope to have more work published in the future. I hate the bio I wrote for myself to go along with it. It's too much.

9.26.2019

BB was pretty heartbroken yesterday when she found out her third child is going to be her third boy. I really feel for her. I felt the same way when Aaliyah turned out to be a girl. I know when that little bundle gets here (and probably before), the disappointment will fade, like it did for me. I am actually very happy to have three girls, and with Q, I have a son.

9.27.2019

I'm getting my wisdom tooth pulled in a couple of hours. It really needs to come out, so I guess I'm ready to get this done, but my anxiety has been slowly creeping up the closer I get to my appointment. I haven't eaten today, and I'm starting to get irritable. I spent most of the morning giving the house a deep clean and putting up my fall stuff. I even cleaned up the porch and the yard. How come my family won't pop up now when the crib looks great?

9.28.2019

My wisdom tooth that has been bothering me on and off for several years and that I attempted to get removed twice—both in vain—is finally out of my mouth. I was pretty anxious when I was waiting in the office, but my surgeon was really fast, and I was super numb. I don't really have a fear of needles and pain at the dentist; it's more a fear of what the numbing meds will do to my body. The whole left side of my face was numb, even my ear. It was really trippy.

Miyah had soccer today, and she did really good. I love seeing her aggressive side come out.

9.29.2019

I'm happy today. Despite my mouth being swollen and in a bit of pain, I am enjoying my Sunday. Yoga was great. I got a new plant I've been lusting over from Walmart, and I got hubby an aloe plant (the aloe he bought me drowned outside). I am looking forward to my writer's meeting in a couple hours. My room smells good, and I organized and dusted it, making it feel like an oasis.

9.30.2019

Believe it or not, I didn't realize the kids were off today for Rosh Hashanah. I'm still making the same mistakes I made last school year that really screwed a lot of things up. My mouth is still pretty raw on the inside, but I'm maintaining and have gotten over the fear of taking several different medications in one day. I'm on pain meds and antibiotics on top of my daily meds. When September started, I couldn't imagine how it would end or how I would feel. I'm not the Dana I was before my accident. I keep waiting for her to return, but maybe I will never be that Dana again. Maybe that's how it's supposed to be.

2019

Currently

LOVING my journey. despite the rough terrain

MAKING food for the soul. but not food

READING not enough. but I have good books waiting

THINKING about the holidays

EATING lots of junk

WISHING for happiness always

HATING obsessive and negative thoughts

PLANNING a few things

DRINKING water

WANTING success

10.1.2019

Hello, October. I'm going back to work soon. I put in my first application already, and I have a few more to fill out. I'm excited to get back into the workforce and scared at the same time. What I'm really looking forward to is being able to buy things for myself, the household, or even my husband without having to worry if I'm going to put us in a bind.

10.2.2019

I think I may need to go up a dose with my meds. I've been obsessing over having a panic attack seizure for the past twenty-four hours and only because someone told me they used to have them, which has nothing to do with me. This type of behavior is not OK. I'm trying to challenge these irrational, negative thoughts, but my body is already going into fight-or-flight mode. Will this cycle ever end?

I took Angel to a music class, and she loved it so much. She asked the teacher if she knew any songs about animals, and Ms. Gina strummed her guitar and sang, and Angel danced around as if she was floating on air. I had to hold back tears. My daughter looked so free. I long to be that free.

10.3.2019

Why do terrible things happen to innocent people? Why do people suffer and starve? I must remind myself that I am blessed to have a roof over my head and plumbing and food.

And my husband and children and I are healthy. I need to be grateful. Rough day. I had to take an Ativan. Felt shameful that I had to. I called my psychiatrist, and she made me feel better.

10.4.2019

Today is better than yesterday but still not good. I had a very rough morning with bouts of panic. I have spent a lot of time online, looking at reviews for my meds. I kind of want to stop taking them. But then, I think of how I was before. I was terrified to eat my food. I couldn't enjoy my vacation because I was too far away from home. I'm just scared I won't ever really be better.

10.5.2019

Today was better. Miyah had soccer this morning, and we went to a fall festival afterward. I tried to stay in the moment, but negative thoughts would creep in, causing moments of fear. I fought through it, though. I went for a nice walk, and the silence and open air was good for me. Irshaad is going back to work on Monday, and I'm happy because he's been out for a while, and I know our finances were starting to stress him out. But I'm nervous to be alone again.

10.6.2019

The baby had me up at all hours last night and into the wee hours this morning. I slept in and didn't go to yoga, but I woke up feeling disoriented. I felt OK as far as anxiety goes, but then, my thoughts started coming back to me again. I'm trying to stay busy today. I recently joined a few Facebook groups for people who are on sertraline, like myself, but it is both inspirational, with people sharing their success stories, and triggering, with people suffering for weeks and months while adjusting and having to up their doses over and over. I started a messenger chat with four other women who are all early into their journeys. It's encouraging, but I wonder if I'm doing more harm than good. I don't know, but it's good to know others are going through this rough-ass time. And I can be grateful because some have it worse than me.

10.7.2019

I just ate a bagel. I used to avoid them because they're so big, bulky, and hard to get into really small pieces to swallow. I actually was able to eat without a fear of choking. It's probably been about a year since I've been able to do this. A small and important victory. I'm still feeling bouts of anxiety throughout the day, and it sucks. I see my psychiatrist tomorrow, so I'm hopeful she can help me come to some conclusions. On a positive note, baby Aaliyah is walking! She's been taking a few steps here and there for a while, but now, she is walking, with her cute little baby self.

10.8.2019

I saw my therapist and psychiatrist today. I cried to both of them about how frustrating this whole process has been. They both encouraged me. My therapist said she shared my article with some of her colleagues, and she's proud of me. She told me to try a visualization technique. I think I will. My psychiatrist wants me to up my dose again to double what it is now, which is still a small dose for anxiety. I'm scared of the side effects. I just want to be better. I just want to wake up and feel normal. I just want the meds to help me without hurting me first. I'm going to start the new dose in two days. Irshaad will be home with me in case anything happens. Before I left my psychiatrist, she gently told me, "You're a strong person." I hope it's true.

10.9.2019

The kids were off today. We were pretty busy; we went to Angel's music class, Aaliyah's one-year checkup, and went to hang with BB and the kids. I was a bit anxious throughout the day, but I kept checking in with the girls in my sertraline chat, and they made me feel better. We are all at different doses and stages of our meds, but we're all going through the same thing. Also, my family is broke as hell. Thank God Irshaad went back to work again.

10.10.2019

I started my new dose today, and I had an OK day. I'm thinking tomorrow and the next couple of weeks won't be so easy-breezy, though.

10.11.2019

I am starting a challenge for myself. Thirty days in a row of at least fifteen minutes of meditation. Angel and Aaliyah took a nap today, and I tried the visualization technique while doing some yoga poses, and when I finished, my anxiety was gone.

10.12.2019

I went out to the library and to run some errands. I meditated and did yoga before dinner while trying to drown out Aaliyah whining in the background, but I got through it fine. It really is good for my mental health.

10.13.2019

I did my usual Sunday routine. I have a few chores I need to catch up on, which I have no desire to do. The kids have no school tomorrow. I feel pretty OK today.

10.14.2019

I didn't do anything today. My girls asked me if we could go to the park or the elementary school to play, and I said no, even though I think I should have taken them. I just didn't have the drive to do anything other than sit on the couch, lay in bed, and watch YouTube videos. I still had to clean and look after the children, but I felt a bit useless today, like I wasn't the greatest mom. I'm still meditating; it's going well.

Lynn

That happened to me when I was on Effexor. I was on 150 mg and got off. When I got back on, I had to go up to 225 mg for it to be effective.

Dana

I wasn't on this high of a dose last time, either. I'm different now, worse than I was before.

Lynn

How long have you been on it now? After how many weeks did you move up?

Dana

I was right at three weeks and a couple of days for 50.

Lynn

Did you start at 25? If so, for how long?

Dana

Yes, for a month.

Lynn

So you were on lower doses for about seven weeks before moving up, Dana?

Dana

Well, three to four weeks per dose. Basically every time I have seen my doctor, she has upped me. I see her once a month.

Jane

I upped within a week. 50 to start. Next week, 100. A week after, 150. Then, to 200. I don't think there's a right or wrong way to how slow you go up. Maybe just how well you handle the side effects?

Lynn

I finally got rid of the side effects; now, it's just anxiety. I'll give it a couple more weeks. I've been sleeping OK.

10.16.2019

I'm still meditating, although I only did it for five minutes today, and it's starting to feel like a chore.

10.17.2019

I can't wait for Friday.

10.18.2019

I've put in a ton of applications and haven't gotten a single call back. I was really anticipating my phone to be ringing off the hook with offers. I applied to mostly retail jobs and even fast food, and not a single fuck has been given, apparently. I might just bite the bullet and call McDonald's. I feel like they would hire me and have me working the quickest. And funnily enough, out of all the places I've applied to, McDonald's pays the most.

10.19.2019

Community Day was at the park today, and Miyah, Angel, and I tore the place up. The weather was crisp but not too chilly. I got to wear a new outfit I bought during my "shopping spree." It's nice to have cute clothes ready to go that actually fit my body. I felt pretty. Unfortunately, before I actually took the girls to the park, I felt anxious like old Dana. I didn't eat, and I had to do a lot of deep breathing. I used to think I didn't have social anxiety, but maybe I do. We met Fatima and her kids at the park, and for some reason, that made me nervous, even though *I* invited *them,* and I see her pretty often at this point. I did not like how I felt, stressing out until we got there, but the feeling did go away.

10.20.2019

I got a ton of shit done today—laundry, cleaning, dishes, my hair, Miyah's hair, dinner, and folding clothes, and I did it without getting too upset, annoyed, or frustrated with the kids. And my husband was in bed all day with a cold. I think the time I took to lock myself in the girls' room and meditate for fifteen minutes when the baby was napping helped chill me out. I am proud of myself for trying my best to take care of my mental health. That is real self-care. I didn't get to journal or read or catch up on my shows, but I have a lot of things to do during my free time throughout the week.

10.21.2019

Aaliyah has an ear infection. The thick pink meds her pediatrician prescribed transported me back in time. All those memories of being a child and having my own mom administer this medicine came flooding back to me. It's funny how smells can trigger memories we forgot we had.

10.22.2019

Angel started story time today. I get a kick out of seeing her interact with other kids. Aaliyah is now at the age where she's very demanding and throws herself back and forth when she doesn't get what she wants, and she did a lot of that today. I had a meeting with Q's teachers and guidance counselor. I hope I didn't look as uncomfortable as I felt. I left the meeting feeling hopeful.

10.23.2019

My therapist recommended a book to me, and I requested it from the library. I started reading it last night, and it's basically a self-help book on how to cope with anxiety and other "mental disorders." I'm hopeful these techniques will help me. I still can't believe my anxiety has come to this place. When I was on my meds before, everything was so uncomplicated. Now, I really have to work to keep myself sane. Yoga, journaling, and meditation have been helping me find peace, and I've been reading for pleasure as well. As always, I remain hopeful that everything will be alright soon.

10.24.2019

Congratulations on being six months sober, Mama. I know it isn't easy.

10.25.2019

Another week has gone. I made a few calls, trying to follow up on a couple of places I applied to, but I hit some roadblocks. Next week, I will continue to follow up and maybe go to a few places in person. I really thought I would have a job by now. Thankfully, Irshaad is back out and making good money, but even with his top rate, we are constantly playing catch up, and we're continuing to live paycheck to paycheck. I cannot wait to contribute to this household and take some weight off his shoulders.

10.26.2019

We had Trunk or Treat today. Miyah's Scary Spice costume was adorable, although I'm not sure anyone recognized who she was, but she looked so cute! I'm proud that my little brown girl picked a brown woman to dress up as because "she's so pretty and cool." Girl Power! I wanted to make Angel's butterfly costume and give her wings that could flap, but she fell in love with store-bought ones, and I was able to add some flare for her. Aaliyah was very pleasant the entire time; she was just taking everything in and fell asleep on the walk home. Last year, at this time, I carried her in a body snug, and she remained covered and slept the entire time. I wonder how next year will be for us, although she'll probably still be in a stroller.

10.27.2019

I need to have some more me-time this week. Meditating has been helping me center myself and improve my mood, but I still can be overwhelmed, especially by the baby. She is still nursing and very clingy. She clings to me often for comfort.

I long for the nights when I can sleep the full way through and not have to whip my boob out on command. I could have stopped by now, but she enjoys it too much, and it provides my last baby with so much comfort. To be honest, it provides me with a lot of comfort as well.

10.28.2019

I am currently at the library. Dinner is cooked, and the kids and hubby are fed. I have about an hour until I have to pick up Q from practice and run to the store. I had a rough day. I was so anxious that I almost felt dizzy. I powered through it, but it was hard to distract myself. I followed up with a store I applied to and spoke to a manager today, but he told me they were all set. I think I'm going to do the same with McDonald's tomorrow. Another month is almost over, and I wonder where I will be mentally this time next month.

10.29.2019

I woke up feeling fine today and had an absolutely unremarkable day. I barely got to see my husband because he had work and school and ran errands in between. I took Aaliyah and Angel to story time at the library. A little boy kept trying to rudely move Angel out of the way, and she told him off. I'm so proud of her; she is so tough. I've been reading a lot lately and really enjoying it. I'm still meditating and loving that as well. I think I want to challenge myself to do something else before 2020.

10.30.2019

I was crazy anxious again today. Angel's music class was canceled, but I still needed to get out of the house to distract myself and cheer her up. We went to Dollar Tree, and she picked out a toy and a treat. Then, we did some window shopping at a few stores because I am redecorating our bathroom. We stopped at McDonald's, then went home. Being out and about helped. Now, I'm back home and feeling crummy again. Off to go meditate.

10.31.2019

I'm tired, but I haven't meditated yet, and I need to take a shower, too. I stayed up while everyone else went to bed, which I haven't done in a long time. The house was a tornado of clothes, candy wrappers, and bags from my shopping trip earlier. Angel and I went to a few stores today, and I wish I made her stay home so I could enjoy my time in solace. I always feel guilty for not giving the girls enough of my time, so I chose to "be a good mom" instead of taking care of my mood and health. It was the baby's first official Halloween, and she was a bumblebee. Miyah was Scary Spice, Angel was a butterfly, and Q wore an eerily serene white mask. I was reminded throughout the night that I need to go to the dentist ASAP. I need to take better care of myself in every way I can. Happy Halloween.

november

2019

Currently

LOVING me

MAKING some positive steps. I think

READING some pieces that have inspired me

THINKING about who I inspire

EATING well

WISHING I was stronger

HATING self-doubt

PLANNING for the holidays

DRINKING the usual

WANTING the usual

FEELING curious

11.1.2019

November, huh? This year is going to be over in the blink of an eye. I have found a new challenge for myself. I am doing NaNoWriMo this year, which is basically a month-long sprint to fifty thousand words for your novel. I participated in 2017 and actually hit fifty thousand words. I started my story today, and it's one I've been internalizing for a while, with some biographical elements to it. I called Starbucks to get an update on my application status and spoke to the manager. She asked me to email her with my availability and a little about myself. I have experience working for Starbucks, so I hope that helps me stand out as a candidate. She said they will be doing phone interviews this weekend, and they will call me back.

11.2.2019

Call me Macaulay Culkin because I'm home alone! I've been in a very playful mood lately, and my children are loving it. Hubby took all the children out of the house to run errands and see their granny; they were very excited. I just took an amazing shower in our newly decorated bathroom of royal purple and gold. It feels luxurious and peaceful. Miyah's last soccer game was this morning, and it was a parents versus kids game. I was sitting in the car feeding the baby at first (because it was very cold, not because I'm ashamed to nurse in public). When I finished up and found Miyah on the field, her face lit up. It was one of those moments where you realize how significant you are to someone else. I have a ton of stuff on my to-do list. I meditated and did laundry earlier in the day, but I have a ton of words I'm supposed to be writing for my NaNo story and a stack of books waiting to be read, also three books to finish, applications to continue to fill out, and the mental health workbook is calling my name as well. Clearly, I won't get to all those things tonight or even this weekend.

11.3.2019

I think I landed a job! After reading an ad on Craigslist (I promise this isn't sketchy), I decided to take a chance and drive to the shop, a fairly new mom-and-pop Philly cheesesteak restaurant by my house. I met the owner and spoke to him and his wife, and he really liked me. He said he liked how pleasant I seemed and thought I had a firm handshake (kind of surprising). Unfortunately, the pay isn't great, and there are not that many hours available for me during the week. He did tell me he would figure out something to get me hours because he likes me that much. I left the store feeling really great. The hours are even good enough that I can still go to yoga on Sunday mornings and catch a late-night movie on the weekends if I wanted to.

11.4.2019

So I was called and officially given the job today! The hours are part-time, and the pay is cash plus tips, which works out perfectly. The location is sixty seconds away from my house. I am looking forward to starting this new chapter in my life, and at the same time, I am nervous as hell. This place is a local favorite, with a small staff, and I don't want to screw anything up. My new boss told me they seldom make mistakes, and that worried me a bit because I'm not the most meticulous person in the world. I start in two days, and I'm going to be nervous for some time until I get comfortable. But this is a good nervousness; it's a nervousness that everyone experiences. I can't wait to start bringing a paycheck into my household, and I'm proud of myself for getting my foot in the door. This could be the start of a very productive and fruitful relationship.

11.5.2019

I'm behind on my word count for NaNo. I have to catch up at some point, but I keep letting myself get distracted. I think I'm becoming a bit of a broken record, saying I have so much going on that it's a bit overwhelming. I do know one thing: I am growing more and more sure that this year has been one of the hardest of my life, but it's been absolutely necessary.

11.6.2019

I just got in from my first night of work. I think I did pretty well, all things considered. I am anxious to get my routine down and get comfortable, especially with the cleaning routine and taking orders over the phone. So far, I like my coworkers. It's a small crew, and everyone gets along well, it seems. I look forward to being comfortable and silly with them, too. I think the owners are happy with me, and I am happy with me as well. I'm not ashamed to say I didn't think about the kids one time during my shift, even though I did talk about them. But I felt so loved coming home and seeing their smiling faces at the top of the steps.

11.7.2019

Dana

I see my psychiatrist today. I'm guessing I will be upping my dose yet again.

Jane

What are you on, Dana? I forgot.

Dana

One hundred. Every time I've seen her, we've doubled. 25 to 50. Then, 50 to 100. How long have you been at 200, Jane?

Jane

One month now. Feeling good. I would say she would take you to 150 next, right?

Dana

I'm at the office now. I guess we'll see.

Lisa

Hi, all. Just wondered if any of you get hot hands and feet. I do, especially in the night and first thing in the morning.

Jane

Oh, yes. That's one of my few side effects. Sweaty, sticky hands.

OK, ladies, so I am staying at 100. Doc thinks I'm doing good, and after comparing my irritability, panic attacks, etc., I've improved a lot since the first time I saw her. She said if I need to at some point, we can move up to 150, but I seem to be good here.

Dana

That's great, Dana! I honestly see an improvement in the way you talk since we started. You seem more positive and kind of keep us uplifted.

Samantha

Awesome, Dana. I'm sure with a few more weeks under your belt, you'll be feeling even better.

Jane

Thanks, Jane. I'm happy and relieved. Did you make your appointment to see your specialist yet?

Dana

You girls have been on it the longest; it's about time you start seeing some results.

Samantha

11.8.2019

So work tonight was a bit more challenging than the first one. I made quite a few mistakes writing down tickets and on the register. I feel like I am doing well, but I keep doing stupid things, and being the new person really sucks. I asked my boss if he can give me anything specific he wants me to work on. He just nodded and said that everything will come with time. And he's right. I'm sure a month from now I'll feel a lot better than I do now; going to work won't be this big deal anymore. Speaking of work, Ricky has moved to

Florida to live with Dad, and I was apprehensive for him. But apparently, I was wrong because I am pleased to announce that he is really coming into his own. He has a good job and a car and will be able to get his own place soon. I am so happy for him, and he told me he's proud of how far I've come as well.

11.9.2019

No more soccer for Miyah, but Irshaad is coaching Q's basketball league, as well as playing in the men's league himself. He comes home pretty tired and understandably so, but by then, I need to get out of the house for a while. I reached day thirty of meditation, and this is another victory for me to be proud of. Meditation is a tool I should probably use every single day, and I hope one day I will call on it that often. I had moments during this time period where I was craving the peace and the dark, quiet space (in the girls' room on my yoga mat).

11.10.2019

I worked the day shift today, and I was mostly on my own, but my boss was in the background if I needed help, which I did need because of a few more register mistakes. I did a couple of really dumb things at the beginning of my shift as well, which made me want to crawl under the tiled floor and go away forever! But I left feeling pretty OK. Next week, I will start working alone. I'm nervous already. "A smooth sea does not make a skilled sailor."

11.11.2019

Blah, blah, blah. OK day.

11.12.2019

The first snow of the season started this morning. Angel was disappointed when it quickly melted. She wanted to go outside and play in it, but I assured her she would be able to soon. I spent most of the day feeling anxious, thinking about work tomorrow.

11.13.2019

So I woke up this morning thinking about work today, then suddenly, Irshaad got called into work with no idea when he would be home, and I had to be at my job by four. So I spent a few hours freaking out and reverting to my anxious ways. I didn't eat anything and started worrying about what to tell my bosses and what they might say to me. I called on all available friends to see if they could help, and thankfully, BB came through. I'm annoyed I have been put in this position, but a situation like this was going to happen at some point, and we have to have a plan in place.

11.14.2019

Brought home my first paycheck in almost five years. My husband was proud of me, and although I make in three days what he makes in one shift, I feel good about being able to bring some extra income into the household. We are going to be caught up on all of our bills by next week, and we started buying Christmas presents already. I struggled with some anxiety today when I was in the car running errands. What's the point of being on meds if I'm still suffering from the same shit? I think of what my therapist might say to that. I think I'm going to meditate tonight. I haven't done so since I finished my thirty-day challenge.

11.15.2019

I felt anxious today, but I suffered through it, waiting for work so I could busy myself. Then, when I got to work, I wanted to go home. I went through so many emotions in five hours. I was anxious, silly, embarrassed, awkward, unorganized, overwhelmed, happy, independent, relieved, and busy. Now, I'm home and made it past the initial wave of tiredness. It's two a.m., and I haven't been up this late in a long time. I plan on cleaning my car out tomorrow, bingeing season four of *RuPaul's Drag Race,* and folding massive piles of laundry. Night.

11.16.2019

This Saturday was pretty uneventful, but most are for me, so it's OK. I spent a lot of time folding clothes in front of the television. I did a little shopping to get some things for my car. We got all three girls new car seats, and we bought a new door handle to replace the one Irshaad broke a year ago, so that has inspired me to give the car a really good cleaning and spruce her up. I didn't get around to actually cleaning, but I plan on doing it when I get off of work tomorrow. Irshaad is laid off, and I need to take some time for myself this week to decompress and get some silence. I'm thinking about work tomorrow and hoping I have a day with no accidents. I feel a pressure I haven't felt in a long time. I don't want to disappoint my bosses.

11.17.2019

I had a *long* day at work. We got super busy, and I thought I handled myself quite well. It was my first time truly being by myself. I made a lot of tips! Unfortunately, I did something wrong on the register, and the count was off for the day. My bosses weren't too concerned, but it made me feel like an asshole. Then, I came home and forgot to turn off Irshaad's headlights and killed his car's battery. Why am I so careless? I feel like a kid with the dumb shit I do. Eh. Oh, yeah, and I've completely given up on NaNo. My last word count was around 5K words.

11.18.2019

Today, I was cranky, crabby, and generally unhappy. I was stressed and annoyed, especially with my husband. Luckily, he took it all in stride, but he's partly the reason for my agitation. Every so often, I have to remind him to check on me, to do things for the kids for me, and to even give me a break. And

I get mad at him but don't tell him why I'm mad. I just act passive-aggressive. I know he's not a mind reader. I plan on spending hours at Barnes & Noble tomorrow. Hopefully, it helps lift my mood.

11.19.2019

I am currently sitting at a table in the Barnes & Noble cafe with a cafe mocha and bottled water, my binder spilling with papers, and a couple of books I picked up. The baby had me up off and on all night. I know the time is coming for me to stop nursing her if I want my sanity back. I've gotten a little bit of writing done and found a cute journal for my mom and me. We are going to be journaling together and passing the book back and forth to each other. I'm excited about this. Before I leave, I think I'm going to make another round around this giant corporate bookstore and find a couple of my favorites to read.

11.20.2019

I'm having a hard time properly taking care of myself. I need to eat more. I need to get more alone time and meditate more. I need to take better care of my teeth and skin. I can't keep putting my body and mind last. Yesterday was really incredible for me, with hours of blissful silence, reading, and journaling. The only time I spoke was to order my coffee. I also dressed really nice and put on lipstick. I need more days like yesterday.

Dana Muwwakkil

11.21.2019

I'm tired. Irshaad is at school. The baby cried herself to sleep. Q is sleeping. Tacos are made, and I need to bathe the girls and supervise them while they clean their room. I felt anxious today. I went to the library to start my mother/daughter journal and some reflection questions. I'm still not one hundred percent better, but I won't burden anyone else with this information. Now, I'm going to meditate for about ten minutes and go back into mommy mode.

11.22.2019

In an hour, I will be starting my shift for the night, and I have dreaded it all day. I have got to get over this. I don't even work twenty hours a week, but I spend just as much time stressing about my job. I was just starting to feel comfortable and confident in the front, then on Wednesday, they decided to cross-train me in the back. Now, I feel brand new again. Irshaad went food shopping for Thanksgiving with Angel. The baby slept, so I had a lot of quiet time, and I tried to enjoy it, but I kept waiting for them to come back home. I kept looking out the window to see if Irshaad was here. I think I may need to up my dose on this medicine, but I don't want to.

11.23.2019

Everyone has fallen asleep, and I will join them shortly. I was having a pretty good day until my boss texted me asking if I can come in early tomorrow for a work meeting. Then, the thoughts started. I'm a screwup. I suck at my job. My coworkers think "X" about me. Customers think "Y" about me. Then, my boss texted me back that the meeting was canceled.

I got Miyah and Angel ready for the movies, and I started stressing and getting annoyed and mean as usual. And I wondered to myself, *Is this normal?* I was like this before, miserable when trying to get my kids dressed for an event in an allotted time. So am I better, worse, or the same? We went to the movies, and I felt better as soon as we got in the car. The rest of my day was fine. Goodnight.

11.24.2019

I just got home from work, and I'm exhausted. I fucked up on the register *again*, doing the same exact thing I did last week by hitting a certain button (on their ancient register) that did something really weird. Other than that, I don't think I made any errors, but the one I made was a big one, and it messed with my confidence. I wonder when I'll stop sucking at my job.

11.25.2019

Miyah had a half-day today because of parent-teacher conferences. Her teacher said she loves Miyah, and she's very sweet and affectionate. She also said she's working at grade level and beyond, which was nice to hear. I asked how she was doing socially, and she said Miyah is painfully shy in the classroom and only recently opened up to her teacher. I need to help my baby break out of her shell. Being an introvert is OK, but I want my Mimi to feel confident and self-assured. Hard to teach her to be the things I am not.

11.26.2019

Miyah and Q both had half-days today. Irshaad and I have been cleaning since we woke up. His mother is coming over on Thursday for Thanksgiving and maybe his brothers as well. The house currently looks like a tornado hit it, but it is organized chaos. We have not hosted Thanksgiving in years, nor have we cooked a turkey in years, but I'm confident we're going to have a yummy meal. I'm making a baked mac and cheese recipe I always use, and we're making homemade mashed potatoes, which are so good. I can't wait for the turkey and gravy and Hawaiian rolls, too.

11.27.2019

I didn't have to go to work today. I was relieved, but my paycheck is going to be pretty pathetic next week. It's OK, though, I had some baking to do, and we still had cleaning to get done. I think I'm going to do some Black Friday shopping. I'm a little nervous, but I think I might have a good time. Yes, I know that sounds ridiculous.

11.28.2019

Happy Thanksgiving! Today was pretty darn good. I was a little tense while Irshaad and I were cooking, but I never got stressed out, I never lashed out, and we had a great time. Irshaad's mom and brothers came over, and we all enjoyed the food and each other's company. I went to Walmart to get Q a TV for Christmas and a few things for the girls. It was chaotic, but I got the items I wanted. I'm eating some pumpkin pie and drinking a big cup of soda. Goodnight!

11.29.2019

Self-Discovery Questionnaire:

Question 11: Write down your top ten goals you want to achieve by the end of the year.

1. Be in a good place mentally
2. Financial independence
3. Start a new fitness journey (muscle building)
4. Eat more nutritiously and drink more water
5. Complete *The Anxiety Diaries*
6. Take better care of my skin and teeth
7. Give myself quiet time every day
8. Finish the first draft of *What They Know about Me*
9. Keep up with friend mail
10. Try and maintain organization

11.30.2019

The girls and I put up our Christmas decor today, and I baked some brownies and cookies. Fatima is having a girls' night get-together, and I'm going to start getting ready for it in about an hour. I'm a little nervous about the party, even though I'm sure it's going to be fun. I can be awkward in social situations, especially with new people. Anyway, I plan on letting loose, drinking, and having fun. Goodnight, November.

december

2019

Currently

LOVING what meditation is doing for me

MAKING changes that need to be made

READING works from Roxane Gay

THINKING too much about 'what if'

EATING still working on getting more nutrition.

WISHING for my low points to stay behind me

HATING that little voice

PLANNING Don't call it a comeback.

DRINKING some water but perpetually dehydrated

WANTING to not question how I'm feeling

FEELING thankful, hopeful, and curious

12.1.2019

December needs no introduction. I bought myself a new planner today, and instead of waiting until January to start making some changes, I decided I would start early. I want this last month to be productive and organized, and I want to make more holiday memories with my kids. Last night, I had a ball at Fatima's girls' night. I did have moments of awkwardness, but it felt great to get out, be around women, have girl talk, drink, and be silly. I need more nights like this in 2020.

12.2.2019

It's a snow day. Can you tell I need some me-time since I'd rather sit in the empty laundromat because it's warm and quiet than go home? I wanted to go to the library and write for a couple of hours, but it's closed today. This silence feels so good. I'm doing some extra day shifts at my job this week since Irshaad is still out of work. I was hoping my income could be extra for Christmas shopping and to catch up on bills, but since he's only collecting unemployment, we're still just breaking even. I know all this struggling won't be forever, and I know somehow we're going to be able to give the kids a great Christmas and pay our bills. So for that, I am thankful.

12.3.2019

I was very anxious today while at work and at home afterward. I shouldn't be like this still. These meds should have steadied by now, which makes me think I may need to go up on my dose. I hate this so much. I just want to feel like I did before the meds on a regular day.

12.4.2019

I am working a ten-hour shift today. My paycheck next week is going to be so lovely. Even though I know what I'm doing at work and am comfortable with my coworkers, I still find myself getting nervous because of the unknown. I just need to get over it. This job has been such a blessing for myself and my family. It's so close and convenient, and they work with me on my hours. I need to stop stressing so much. I'm worried that I've shaved years off of my life with all this worrying. I see my psychiatrist tomorrow and will see what she says about this dose and possibly going up.

12.5.2019

So after working that ten-hour shift yesterday, I can finally say I feel quite comfortable doing my job and am doing it kind of well. I was off today and saw my psychiatrist. She doesn't think I need to up my dose and reminded me that it's normal to be up and down. And I do get that, but will I ever be just stable? I'm trying my best to take care of myself and drink enough water and eat right. I actually just remembered I've been forgetting to take my weekly vitamin D pill. Going to do that now.

12.6.2019

I worked another *long* shift today, and boy, are my puppies howling. I feel like I'm now comfortable with my coworkers and what I'm doing. I want to read, watch videos, and hang out with my daughters, but I can't get out of this bed. I have a newfound respect for what my husband does when I'm at home. I hope it's vice versa. I think it is.

12.7.2019

I need to meditate, but I'm not going to until I get home from Mason's birthday party. My patience is thin, and I had a lot on my to-do list, and I need some silence. But for now, the shower will suffice. Hopefully, spending time with BB will lift my mood.

12.8.2019

I woke up at 7:30 this morning, had my coffee and something to eat, and went to a very crowded yoga class. The instructor was different, and the class was challenging but satisfying. I ran out to the bank afterward, then went back home to change and visit with my family before work. I was training the new daytime girl, and I felt a lot of pressure to train her the right way, which made my job a lot more stressful, but at least I can teach her in a way I wish I was taught. Our day was long and quite hellish, but I never lost my cool, and I came home feeling even-tempered, although exhausted. I feel quite good, actually.

12.9.2019

I have been using my new planner to keep track of daily tasks and appointments again. I'm really trying to practice mindfulness and good nutrition, and writing and reading are a big part of that for me. I've been obsessed with guided journals lately and can't wait to buy myself some. I've been very productive since Miyah went to school this morning. I did my annual toy purge, decluttered and organized my closet and the linen closet, and did lots of cleaning. I felt pretty anxious today for no reason at all. Something must be wrong with these meds, and it makes me so sad that 2019 is coming to an end, and I still feel like this.

12.10.2019

I'm supposed to go to work today to do some more training for the new girl, but Irshaad got called into work today for a one-day job, which is fine, but I left the new girl hanging. I think she was alone, and I know she was not ready. I hope her day was OK. I am looking forward to going back to my old shift after this week.

12.11.2019

Going to work in a couple of hours. I have been trying to be present and in the moment with Angel and Aaliyah and play with them, then have some alone time before I have to leave. I'm almost done with my Christmas shopping. I cannot wait for my yearly ritual of excitedly gathering all the items each

Dana Muwwakkil

kid is getting and wrapping everything nice and pretty while watching a Christmas movie and drinking coffee.

12.12.2019

So the new girl quit. She said the job was giving her anxiety. I feel really bad because I think she wasn't given enough training. I think if I had gotten the chance to work with her on Tuesday or even on Wednesday during the day, she would have felt a lot more comfortable. I mean, it took me weeks and weeks until the thought of work didn't cause me to shit a brick.

12.13.2019

I worked another ten-hour shift today. I am tired. I saw a new side of my boss tonight. He banged his fist against the takeout window in anger over something trivial. He wasn't directing the anger at me, but it was shockingly innapropriate. Goodnight.

12.14.2019

BB and I took our kids to see Eggbert today, per our annual holiday tradition. I sent pictures to Ricky, my mom, and Drea. It made us all feel nostalgic. It's so important to make these memories with my children. Then, Irshaad and I took all our babies to our friends' house for their kid's birthday party. I also sent out some Christmas cards and mail to some family and friends. I hope getting some snail mail makes them smile.

12.15.2019

I held back tears at work today when my teenage coworker, a total sweetheart, told me she read my essay about my anxiety and was glad she read it because her boyfriend suffers from similar anxiety. We talked briefly about my mental health history and about being on meds and my CBT (cognitive-behavioral therapist). She said she thinks I'm strong to be able to share my story and help others. I thanked her, feeling proud. But I was too bashful to tell my boss that I suffer from anxiety when they were talking about why the new girl quit.

12.16.2019

I took myself out on a little date this morning. I went to Barnes & Noble. I ate decadent chocolate cheesecake and drank a cafe mocha. I spent a lot of my time looking at guided journals and new planners. I bought a daily one for the new year. It's leather bound and beautiful. I felt guilty for being out of the house, even though it was only for a couple of hours on the only day I have off until Saturday. It's supposed to snow tomorrow. Hopefully, I have a short day.

12.17.2019

OK, I am finally starting to miss my children when I am at work. I am finally longing to be home. I am finally cherishing the days at home when I would call myself bored. I come home exhausted and not really up for anything other than lying in bed. I asked my boss if I could have the day off for

Christmas Eve, and he said he will think about it. It kind of threw me because I have been working so hard for him. Tsk, tsk, it's almost 2020, and I still don't have a backbone.

12.18.2019

I had my first asshole customer at work today. I've dealt with people who aren't very polite or even nice, but I actually had someone that was rude to me, and he made me uncomfortable. Despite his rudeness, I kept it professional, but his attitude never ceased. The interaction put me in a bit of a mood for the rest of the day. If I'm being honest, I think my reaction to the situation has to do with my desperation to be well liked.

12.19.2019

I brought Angel with me to work today. I really appreciate that I can bring my kids to work if I want to. Miyah had a class party today, but I wasn't able to attend because I asked to sign up too late. Her teacher told me I can come to the Valentine's Day party. I'm just worried that, by then, Irshaad will be back to work, and I won't be able to attend because of the younger children, which is usually the situation.

12.20.2019

Well, it happened. I cried at work today. I asked my boss once again if I could have Christmas Eve off or even leave early that day, and he flatly told me no. When I told him I was disappointed because I wanted to spend the day with my children, his response was, "We all do." And I just couldn't hold back the tears because, honestly, it hurt my feelings. The day of Christmas Eve isn't even a day in my typical work schedule. I have just been filling in for the past couple of weeks. I have seen a side of him I don't like, and it was really quite cold. I came home and didn't tell Irshaad. I didn't want to tell him I cried at work. I don't want him to hate my boss, either.

12.21.2019

My other boss called me this morning and told me I can have tomorrow off. That instantly perked me up because I have three days off in a row to spend with my family and get stuff done. I'm sure she heard about the crying fiasco, and I'm still embarrassed, but it is what it is. I wear my heart on my sleeve.

12.22.2019

I was holding my breath all day, hoping my last package of presents would come in. It kept getting delayed. I went to the mall to pick up a dress I accidentally had shipped there for Angel, then I picked up another outfit for Q and two more controllers for the girls' Wii we bought them. I saw BB for a quick second. I'm using her springform pan to make a Christmas cheesecake. I haven't made anything from scratch since the Super Bowl, so I hope it's tasty. I'm excited to bake and spend time with the girls tomorrow, but I also have a long day of cleaning and organizing.

12.23.2019

Something is wrong with me. I spent all weekend looking for a bag of goodies my mom sent the girls and me for Christmas. After pulling everything out of my closet and rearranging, I came to the conclusion that I must have thrown it out. I went armed with some of Irshaad's gloves and found the bag unharmed at the top of our trash can outside (I also almost busted my ass on ice). My mom sent me a scarf; it's pink, fuzzy, and soft like a shag rug. It smelled like her, and I sniffed it for a long time, missing her. I had a busy day of laundry, doing the girls' hair, organizing, and preparing for tomorrow so I can just come home from work and enjoy my family and make the cheesecake. I am exhausted.

12.24.2019

I just got home from working a three-and-a-half-hour shift. My boss is also giving me the day after Christmas off as well. I can't tell you how much of a fool I feel like for crying. I still have some prepping to get done for tomorrow's festivities. I'm making baked ziti tonight and brownies and cheesecake, and I can't wait to eat it tomorrow. I am so excited to see my children's smiling faces in the morning.

12.25.2019

It's early evening on Christmas, and I'm emotionally burnt out, physically exhausted, and, to be honest, a little grumpy. The girls and I had a great morning with Irshaad, playing games and opening toys. Q came home around noon, and as a stepmama, he gave me such a high compliment on all his gifts. And my cheesecake turned out wonderful. But as the day has gone on, I've grown tired and cranky, and my patience has worn thin again. I need to go to a dark room and meditate. I need to journal and let my thoughts soar. I must get up and take care of myself before the night is over. Make it my gift to myself. Merry Christmas.

12.26.2019

I was getting ready to go run some errands when I suddenly felt a wave of panic come over me for no reason at all. The feeling kept coming back for hours, even as I was driving, which I forced myself to do. By noon, I decided to stick with my plan to go to the library and write. I still felt anxious, but it subsided for the most part. I came home and tried to prepare the household since I'm going to be working for the next three days. It's now 4:30, and my boss just asked me if I could work tonight. I did not want to say yes. I was just about to go meditate in the girls' room, then play Mario Party with them on the Wii we just bought. There is so much more I want to say, but I will wait.

12.27.2019

More anxiety today. Really bad day. Work was long as hell, and my anxiety was so bad, I had a hard time speaking. I am home and mentally, emotionally, and physically exhausted. Praying tomorrow is better. I don't know how much longer I can do this.

12.28.2019

I felt fine today, although I woke up afraid I would have another bad day. I had work again, and it was a pretty normal day for me. I'm sad this year is coming to an end, and I'm still struggling with my anxiety, still unsure of what I will do in terms of medication.

12.29.2019

I woke up after getting plenty of rest last night and went to yoga. I was worried all morning about my anxiety returning today, which was really all I could think about. I brought Miyah and Angel to work with me, and they had fun, although they got bored after a couple of hours. A couple of hours into my shift, my anxiety returned. I couldn't stop clenching my damn jaw; it was hell! I think I'm going to call my doctor tomorrow and tell her what's going on. Tomorrow is my only day off for the next couple days, and I have a lot of tasks to complete, so I'm still getting up in the morning with the intention of having a good day and accomplishing my daily goals.

12.30.2019

Today was good and bad at points. I had a lot of tasks to complete today, and I got them all done, but I was stressed throughout the day. I really don't want to go to work tomorrow, but I am. I never called my doctor today, but I might call her tomorrow. We'll see. One more day until the end of the year. Also the end of the decade.

I'm at a party right now. There are a couple of hours until midnight. I feel good. I look good. I'm with my wonderful family and friends. I've seen a lot of people reflecting, not only on the year but the decade, which is about to end. In the last ten years, I started a relationship with the love of my life, who became my husband. I started the transition from a single young woman to wife and mother, and the change seemed to be smooth at first, but in time, I have lost myself in motherhood. One thing that has followed me like a dark cloud all throughout this past decade, which finally took hold of me this year, was my anxiety. It went from creeping up on me from time to time to becoming a constant and even daily struggle because I never properly addressed it before.

I know not everyone reading this will agree with me for turning to medication for my anxiety, and that is OK. I'm still searching for the answers and striving for my complete mental wellness. I was bummed about not ending this diary the way I would end a satisfying novel, with a truly happy ending and all my questions answered. But the truth is my story isn't a work of fiction, and that's the good thing about it as well. This is my story and my life, and I am in control. This is only the beginning.

"We are powerful because we have survived."
-Audre Lorde

MENTAL HEALTH RESOURCES

If the situation is potentially life threatening, get immediate emergency assistance by calling 9-1-1, available 24 hours a day.

Text HOME to 741741

https://www.crisistextline.org/

National Suicide Prevention Lifeline: 1-800-273-TALK (8255)

SAMHSA Treatment Referral Helpline: 1-877-SAMHSA7 (1-877-726-4727)

Get general information on mental health and locate treatment services in your area. Speak to a live person, Monday through Friday from 8 a.m. to 8 p.m. EST.

https://www.mentalhealth.gov/

ABOUT THE AUTHOR

Dana Muwwakkil is a proud black scribe, poet, and mother of four. She enjoys dark chocolate and coffee while she writes about mental health, motherhood, and the awkward situations she seems to find herself in. *The Anxiety Diaries* is her first book.

Thank you for reading *The Anxiety Diaries: Volume 1*
If you enjoyed this book, please help spread
the word by leaving an online review.

CONNECT WITH
DANA MUWWAKKIL

Website: www.theanxietydiaries.com
Facebook: Dana Muwwakkil
Instagram: @doesanyonewritelettersanymore

Made in the USA
Middletown, DE
18 October 2020